WHO CALLS THE TUNE?

Psychodrama draws on a combination of role play and the challenge of the unpredictable. Although more commonly used with adults, it had its genesis in children's play. In *Who Calls the Tune?* Bernadette Hoey explains how its powerful techniques can be safely used in working with the child who has been badly traumatized. Children encountering therapy are often wary. By playing as an equal, but also as an adult responsive to the healing qualities of play, the therapist permits the balance of power to shift unobtrusively backwards and forwards with the child, whilst respecting the boundaries the child may wish to keep. Thus sometimes the therapist 'calls the tune' of the play and sometimes the child. Therapist and child enter together a world of play that can be unpredictable, funny and moving – an apparently spontaneous form of healing.

Beginning with an examination of the ideas of Jacob Moreno as they relate to children, the book goes on to detail the author's own development of psychodramatic techniques using puppets, soft toys, stories and poems. Providing practical examples of work with children suffering from a range of problems, including language disorder, depression and abuse, the author sets her work firmly in the context of theoretical analysis and good practice. Her book will be an inspiration to all those who are looking for new ways to help the healing process in troubled children.

Bernadette Hoey is a therapist, trainer and consultant working in private practice.

Photo: Margaret Sail

WHO CALLS THE TUNE?

A psychodramatic approach
to child therapy

Bernadette Hoey

London and New York

First published 1997
by Routledge
11 New Fetter Lane, London EC4P 4EE

Simultaneously published in the USA and Canada
by Routledge
29 West 35th Street, New York, NY 10001

© 1997 Bernadette Hoey

Typeset in Palatino by
RefineCatch Limited, Bungay, Suffolk

Printed and bound in Great Britain by
Biddles Ltd, Guildford and King's Lynn

British Library Cataloguing in Publication Data
A catalogue record for this book is available from the British Library

Library of Congress Cataloguing in Publication Data
Hoey, Bernadette, 1934–
Who Calls the Tune? : a psychodramatic approach to child therapy /
Bernadette Hoey.
p.   cm.
Includes bibliographical references and index.
1. Psychodrama.   2. Child psychotherapy.   3. Psychodrama—Case
studies.   4. Child psychotherapy—Case studies.   I. Title.
RJ505.P89H64   1996
618.92'891523—dc20   96–6387
CIP

ISBN 0–415–14572–4 (hbk)
ISBN 0–415–14573–2 (pbk)

CONTENTS

CONTENTS

ACKNOWLEDGEMENTS

The work behind this book could not have been done without the love, encouragement and support of many people. My first thanks go to my parents, who played with me, and loved me, and encouraged both my creativity and my exploring mind.

My thanks then go to Max Clayton, my principal psychodrama tutor, who gave constructive criticism and encouragement in the early days of this work; to the colleagues who have seen its value and often spent time as sounding boards for me: Pauline Kilby, Margaret Kenny, Dorothea Wagner, Madeline Reid, Jennifer Cavill; to my sister, Anne Hoey, whose clear, analytical mind helped me sharpen the first draft of the book: to those who assisted with the practicalities of producing the manuscript, Gina Louis, The Good Shepherd Social Justice Commission, Irene Bonnici and Judith Boyd (my excellent and ever-patient word processors); The Institute of Human Development (W.A.) at whose mountain retreat the final chapters were written; and so many colleagues who opened their reference libraries to me.

Above all, I thank the children who have allowed me to enter their secret, inner space. I will not forget them.

(As far as possible, I have asked the children who feature in this book for permission to use their stories. Names and identifying details have been changed, but the accounts of actual therapy sessions are true-to-life.)

PHOTOGRAPHS/ ILLUSTRATIONS

The children who appear in these photographs have never engaged in therapy with the author. They have no connection with the stories that appear in this book.

FOREWORD
by
Dr G. Max Clayton

It is with great pleasure that I am writing the foreword to Bernadette Hoey's book. She has dedicated herself to the development of means by which children may experience a renewed love of life, and, in doing so, free themselves from deep-seated pains, anger and despair. She has refused to accept the diminished ability to make satisfying relationships that marks the lives of many children. Nor has she accepted the failure of many children actively to reach forward towards new learning experiences. Her dedication and persistent experimentation have borne fruit, as demonstrated by the release of a renewed enthusiasm for living in the children with whom she has worked. In addition to the direct work with children, she has involved herself in the training of other professionals who are committed to children becoming free from the effects of traumatic events.

The book will have appeal to many different readers. Child therapists will be immediately absorbed by the detailed descriptions of what took place in many sessions with a wide range of children. They will be strengthened and stimulated by the presentation both of theory and of the different techniques used. Parents who read this book will come to recognize afresh the unlimited possibilities for fun, laughter and playful expression in their relationships with their children. Kindergarten and primary school teachers and child-care workers will develop a greater vision of what can be done with children. In fact, any person who is involved with a child in the course of their daily life will develop fresh respect for children and an expanded idea of what a child can accomplish, through reading this book.

All children contain within themselves an inexhaustible source of creative energy. The inventiveness of a child demonstrated in the making up of new games and forms of play is astounding to an observant parent (as well as a source of pride). The vital energy of a child throwing their arms around a parent returning from work can instantly remove the tiredness and drudgery of the day. The truth that comes out of the mouth of a child can stop a person in their tracks and cause them to rethink a course of action. This creative source must be respected if truly therapeutic work is to come about. Such respect is an outstanding feature of every phase of the work done by Bernadette Hoey. It is seen in the preparation done before the first meeting, in the initial greetings and in the structuring and development of each session which are finely tuned to the rhythms of each individual. Her ability to create a structure and offer relevant activities without hesitation in the immediate situation is an inspiration, and the beneficial effect on the development of the child is obvious. But the descriptions and discussions of the work not only inspire, they also contain excellent teaching material which can be immediately applied.

Children are very clear about the type of situation within which they are willing to express themselves. When these conditions do not obtain, no amount of persuasion or cajoling or threats will cause a child to express themselves freely. It is therefore necessary that those who care for and educate children not only know the required type of environment but also develop the attitudes, values and abilities to bring it into being. Each chapter of this book gives valuable clues as to the type of environment within which a child thrives. This includes the physical environment as well as the functioning of the worker.

I have noticed over the years that those people who have developed a good integration of theory and practice develop more effective relationships. The theory has become part and parcel of their actions and speech. They are unified and therefore can express thoughts that are infused with feeling. Children, especially, respond to a well-integrated person who takes thoughtful initiatives and at the same time maintains an emotional link with them. Their basic trust in life is developed through their experience of another human being tuning in with them. Their speech develops through another person's sensitive presence while at the same time using appropriate words. We may say that such a person is being a double for the child. The consistent presence of such a double augments the confidence of a child. The descriptions in this book reveal a well-integrated worker who takes initiatives and uses intelligent speech, and children who blossom in response.

Each example of work includes much improvisation. This improvisation carried through with ease and competence is an important factor in children involving themselves with such a high degree of spontaneity and in letting go of their anxiety and fears. The method of dramatic improvisation described owes much to the work of J. L. Moreno, yet Moreno's teachings have clearly been integrated and developed in an original manner. I feel sure that all of you who read this book will be inspired and will be able to incorporate the principles enunciated into your own theoretical orientation and practice.

This book has been tapping on the walls
of my mind for some years now.
It's time I let it out. It's a book of stories:
the story of how this work developed;
therapeutic stories I've told to children;
and above all, the powerful vignettes
some of them have created as they played
with me, their own stories hidden safely
behind the metaphors.
It is a personal account of the development
of a very interactive work style,
written partly in response to requests
from students who have engaged exuberantly
in training workshops with me.
It is written for them, and for anyone
who is interested in exploring the depth
and variety of children's healing mechanisms.

INTRODUCTION
The Pied Piper

as they reached the mountain-side
A wondrous portal opened wide,
As if a cavern was suddenly hollowed;
And the Piper advanced and the children followed.
(Browning: from 'The Pied Piper')

It was not until 1984 that I discovered psychodrama. I'd heard of it, of course, but it was only in the mid-1980s that I began to study at the Australian College of Psychodrama. And so began the transformation of my work as a therapist. My principal tutor, Dr Max Clayton, had studied under Moreno himself. There was no emphasis in the course on working with children. But Max combined a marvellous sense of play with a sharply penetrating intelligence as he led us into an experiential knowledge of psychodrama in its 'for adults' form. I gradually developed a great wish to trace back, if possible, the connection between psychodrama as we know it today and the early thinking of its founder, Jacob Moreno.

Until very recent months, none of this re-tracing was done through reading. My teachers were the children themselves. Some puppets and dolls had crept in and, over the years, they have multiplied profusely, providing 'auxiliaries' in my psychodramatic play with the children. In a therapy session, I think of myself as a sort of Pied Piper, playing leap-frog with a child. I call a tune. The child begins a game. I follow. At a certain point in the game, as therapist, I take a leap, far ahead of where the child now is. The child is intrigued and leaps forward with a new idea for the game. I follow. And so it goes on.

In about 1908, when Jacob Moreno was a young medical

student at the University of Vienna, he began to play with children at a large public park called the Augarten. This was the beginning of much of the thinking that finally led him to develop the 'creative revolution' of which psychodrama was an integral part. I recently read a description by Moreno of that part of his life and I was delighted to recognize my Pied Piper image.

> One day I walked through the Augarten, a garden near the Archduke's palace, where I saw a group of children loafing. I stopped and began to tell them a story. To my astonishment other children dropped their games and joined in, nurses with their carriages, mothers and fathers and policemen on horseback.
>
> From then on, my favourite pastime was to sit at the foot of a large tree in the gardens of Vienna and let the children come and listen to fairy tales. The most important part of the story was that I was sitting at the foot of a tree, like a being out of a fairy tale, and that the children had been drawn to me as if by a magic flute and removed bodily from their drab surroundings into the fairy land. It was not as much what I told them, the tale itself, it was the act, the atmosphere of mystery, the paradox, the unreal becoming real. I was in the centre, often I moved up from the foot of the tree and sat higher, on a branch; the children formed a circle, a second circle behind the first, a third behind the second, many concentric circles, the sky was the limit.
>
> (Moreno 1934: xviii)

Moreno's magic centred on the tree. Mine centres round the puppets. But what draws the children is a quality from within the therapist. They experience an encounter with an equal, and it takes place within their own world, where fantasy and reality are inextricably entwined, set free by the alchemy of spontaneity.

Working with children involves moving in a world of kaleidoscopic changes, with frames of reference constantly shifting. Nothing is quite as it first seems. The ambiguity of the book's title reflects this. The phrase 'who calls the tune?' refers to a major central theme – namely, the delicate and constantly shifting balance of power that exists between therapist and disturbed child. The child strongly resists abdicating dominion over private inner space, and will not trust a therapist who demands this. The form of therapy described in the book constantly attends to this need of the child, but also takes responsibility for making powerful therapeutic interventions. The therapist is much more than a simple playmate.

The title also hints at the Pied Piper imagery reflected in key illustrations throughout the book. The child in the cover photograph has been interrupted by the sound of the Piper. His face reflects interest, but it also clearly shows his desire for sovereignty over his own life. He will only answer the call when he is certain he can do so on his own terms. He is suspending judgment. The Pied Piper figure in the oak tree links my work with Moreno's early encounters with children. And when the children's voices are to be heard through the narratives of the therapy sessions, they are introduced by the photograph of a girl 'calling a tune' on her recorder, in an atmosphere of freedom.

Browning's Pied Piper found himself seriously at odds with the leaders of Hamelin Town. And political and economic issues find their way, necessarily, into this book also from time to time, for human beings (even the most solitary or self-contained) do not exist in total isolation. Although the primary focus is on the children within the context of the therapy sessions, there is always a recognition that other systems influence their lives – the family (or substitute care); the neighbourhood; the government of the day; the laws of the country; changing world attitudes. For many of the children whose stories appear here, this fabric has been disturbed again and again, causing them to feel powerless actors in a drama that is not of their making.

The book does not attempt a complete overview of the complex social systems that collide with their lives. That would involve intensive research and labyrinthine discussion, resulting in an undue emphasis on the voice of the author. This book is primarily a vehicle for the voices of the children. They have a simplicity and clarity of tone we need to hear. It is essential that we do not crowd them out.

Part I

BACKGROUND

Photo: Tony Terry

1

THEORETICAL FRAMEWORK

> More important than procreation is the child –
> More important than the evolution of creation
> is the evolution of the creator.
>
> (Moreno)

Many years of involvement with children have taught me that, side by side with their candour and simplicity, there can be found within them huge caverns of privacy and a quite complex need to keep at bay any adults who try to push past their protective barriers. This is doubly true in matters concerning their families. 'It's none of your business!' they shout, with their eyes if not their mouths. And most counselling theories for adults taught at our universities and training colleges do not tell us how to enter this very private space. Through psychodrama, I have found a key. The more I have used these methods with children, the more aware I become of the brilliance of Moreno's concepts. He has translated the normal play patterns of children into a complex therapeutic system for adults that opens human experience to unexpected depths. And when the principles of psychodrama are applied back to therapeutic play, the children are unaware of any interruption to their natural form of expression.

There is an air of simplicity in the accounts of actual therapy sessions that appear later in this book. But facilitating such sessions is not quite so simple. A delicate balance needs to be maintained between the roles of alert, analytical therapist and free-wheeling, delighted playmate, both roles coming together in the person who engages so directly with the child. I am aware of many psychodramatists, in several different countries, who are exploring adaptations of psychodrama for children. Their ways of

adapting the method are varied, but certain basic principles underlying their approaches are constant. Little has been written on this
subject, and perhaps it is time to attempt to analyse the particular
adaptation that has unfolded in the course of my own explorations. *How* is it done? What is necessary, what must be avoided,
and how can one remain aware of such issues, while at the same
time maintaining the element of spontaneity so essential to play?
⟍ The relationship and interaction between the child and the
therapist provide the starting-point. No psychodramatic unfolding will happen unless this starting-point includes respect,
equality, openness to the unknown, flexibility and a delight in
play. There *are* skills involved, and the skills must be learned and
practised. But if they are superimposed on an attitude to children
that does not include the foregoing qualities, they will be of little
value, and the therapist will experience frustrating impotence.
This book offers no 'kits and packages', no ready-made formulas.
Skimming through the pages in an attempt to pick out the techniques, without attempting to absorb the philosophy behind
them, will be a useless exercise. 'I can pick the eyes out of a book
quite quickly', a therapist once told me, 'and then I teach the skills
to others, without wading through unnecessary detail'. Well . . .
yes . . . a good expression, 'pick the eyes out': the eyes on their
own have no vision. A therapist who does this goes away with a
method that produces no insights. A bundle of unattached 'skills'
is a dead thing.

MAJOR THEORETICAL INFLUENCES

So, if kits and packages are not here, what is? As we prepare our
minds to examine key concepts further, the questions we ask will
be as important as the facts we discover. Much depends on the
theoretical framework within which a therapist usually works,
with adults as well as with children. In the years before I discovered psychodrama, I was strongly influenced by the writings
of the American psychologist, George Kelly. Kelly (1955) stresses
the importance of recognizing the uniqueness of each person's
view of reality. He sees human beings as scientists, constantly
testing their hypotheses, as they seek to make sense of the world
and all that happens. They end up with a tightly interwoven
system of constructs. Each system is unique to the individual who
created it out of a myriad of idiosyncratic experiences.

Every child a therapist approaches is in the process of constructing such a system. 'Core constructs', for the child, may well be peripheral for the therapist, and vice versa. Core constructs can be changed only when one is ready to make adjustments to the whole interdependent system, and this happens rarely. Defence mechanisms spring into action if one's core constructs are challenged without due notice, or without respect for one's right to retain them. To challenge without respect a child's view of reality is a therapist's path to rejection. The child will immediately become inaccessible – with the tantalizing thoroughness children have perfected when guarding private territory.

Kelly himself insisted on the need for respect. He said that if he was to be remembered at all, he hoped it would not be for having invented his theory of personal constructs, but rather for what he called his 'First Principle'. This was: 'If you don't know what is wrong with the patient, ask him, he *may* tell you' (Kelly 1955:12).

Moreno, of course, was the major influence behind the work described in this book. His method also emphasizes respect. It requires the director to check with the protagonist, seeking clarifying information, whenever in doubt as to significant detail. Moreno calls it 'social investigation'. The whole psychodrama technique depends, for its healing power, on the director's ability to honour the protagonist's inner world and, from within it, to make challenging and extending interventions in a non-manipulative way. Later chapters will expand and develop an understanding of how this is done.

The reader will find in those pages a more extensive exposition of how this particular adaptation of psychodrama developed. Moreno's thinking and my experiential training in his methods were central. But in the actual therapy sessions, the children often took the lead. My explorations were based on what I learnt from them as much as on what I knew. That needs to be remembered. The work of other theorists was never consciously a driving force. Over the years, however, their insights had become part of my tools of trade and, no doubt, they often subconsciously exerted an influence, particularly when instant therapeutic judgments were called for. So there is value in taking the time to make some comparisons with the work of relevant non-psychodrama-based therapists.

COMPARISONS AND CONTRASTS

As an example, let us pursue the theme of respect. Milton Erickson (1958) immediately comes to mind. He was the master of acceptance. The playful ways in which he used children's symptoms and transformed them into a therapeutic game were more than clever. They sprang from his profound acknowledgment of each child's right to his or her existential position.

Virginia Axline (1964) demonstrated a similar sensitivity throughout the whole of her book, *Dibs in Search of Self*. She always totally accepted Dibs's frame of reference. A charming example of this is given in the account of Dibs resisting her invitation to make himself at home. 'Not at home!' Dibs replied, 'at playroom!' 'All right ... make yourself at playroom!' (Axline 1964:122)

Winnicott's description of his work with Iiro (a little Finnish boy suffering from syndactyly) is worth reading in full to gain another perspective on strong but delightfully unobtrusive therapy that accords total respect to the child (Winnicott 1971:12–27). Winnicott distrusted the overt interruption of play by Kleinian psychoanalytic therapists, who put forward their sexually orientated interpretations quite directly to the child. He acknowledged the possibility of error (in content or in timing) on the part of the therapist and he avoided inserting inflexibly stated interpretations into the play. 'Dogmatic interpretation leaves the child with only two alternatives, an *acceptance* of what I have said as propaganda or a *rejection* of the interpretation and of me and of the whole set-up.' (*ibid*:9–10)

In psychodrama, the 'interpretation' is even more oblique. In my work with children, it takes the form, quite often, of *maximizing* a metaphor that seems to me significant or of *doubling* for the protagonist to express, in play, through gesture or strong movement or words, the unstated feeling believed to be behind an imagery-laden action or spoken thought. The child is free to expand the image still further or to make a movement in another direction. Interpretation, in this sense, involves seeing a significance in the child's body language or use of imagery and judging that this instant in the play is highly important. Klein (1932) emphasizes the need for precision and speed in such a moment of judgment, and its place in the case as a whole.

A correct and rapid estimation of the significance of the

material as it is presented at the time, both as regards the light it throws on the structure of the case and its relationship to the patient's affective state at the moment, and, above all, a quick perception of the latent anxiety and sense of guilt it contains – these are the primary conditions for giving the right interpretation, i.e. an interpretation which will come at the right time and will penetrate to that level of the mind which is being activated by anxiety.

(Klein 1932:30)

In my work, this estimation is made partly through knowledge of the child's life history, partly through my understanding of children in general (gained through life experience as well as through the study of child development theories) and partly through observing the child's body language. These tools must be ready to spring to my service in a flash. If they are not operating sensitively at the instant this therapeutic moment appears, then they come too late.

A psychodrama director needs to be able to read body language swiftly and with an enquiring, rather than a judgmental, mind. I recently came across two contrasting descriptions by Freud and by Gestalt therapists who had studied under Fritz Perls.

He that hath eyes to see and ears to hear may convince himself that no mortal can keep a secret. If his lips are silent, he chatters with his finger-tips; betrayal oozes out of him at every pore.

(Freud 1905:94)

The somewhat adversarial tone of this description contrasts with the following comment:

Finally, in Gestalt therapy, much importance is attached to tone of voice, posture, gestures, facial expression, etc., with much of the import and excitement coming from work with changes in these nonverbal communications – transcribing them into type is difficult and loses much of the meaning and immediacy.

(Fagan and Shepherd 1970:x)

The Gestalt theorists' approach is far more in tune with a psychodramatist's reading of body signals. Much of Perls' writing and many of the techniques used by Gestalt therapists are reminiscent of ideas familiar to students of psychodrama (e.g. the 'rehearsal' and 'exaggeration games'; the 'empty-chair' technique; role play, etc.). It was not, therefore, surprising to me to learn that Perls (along with Eric Berne and S.H. Foulkes) had participated in weekly group sessions with Moreno in the 1940s, when similar ideas were first presented. To Moreno's chagrin, however, Perls never acknowledged any debt to his former teacher (Marineau 1989:184).

In my work, this silent language of the body indicates moments of emotional intensity for a child, whether the body speaks with high energy or with a sudden stillness. Unlike Freud, I do not see it as providing me with a means of circumventing a protagonist's wish to hide or to deceive. It is for me more in the nature of a contour map. It allows me to read my way in to understanding this person's inner landscape, or, at least, to make a step towards reaching that goal. This way of working almost certainly would not succeed for a therapist who habitually relies on theories that emphasize power, or distanced analytical judgments, or the use of categorizing labels.

But that is not to dismiss analysis: it is indeed a necessary part of the interactive process that emerges in the course of psychodrama-based play. The therapist must constantly be aware of the child's reactions to any interventions in their shared play, or to words or actions that are part of a therapeutic storytelling process. A sudden widening of the eyes; great stillness; uncomfortable, or very adroit, changing of the subject; a facial expression of peace, intense joy, or relief. All these can be signals that the therapist has correctly guessed key aspects of the child's problem, or that there has been an unknowing stumbling on a painful area the child is not at present prepared to disclose or acknowledge. If these observations are made in the context of a desire to understand the child's own carefully constructed inner world, they will not be experienced as threatening invasions. The delightful shared play can continue even while the therapist is mentally noting the responses and adapting interventions accordingly, moving always with whatever opens out, retaining the memory of insights that have occurred, but not intruding with these insights into the child's play if that play is still unfolding.

Much of the skill involved in such work consists in the therapist's ability to remain spontaneous and open to the unpredictable challenges of the child's play, without abnegating for a moment the role of analytical observer. This involves a curious mixture of following and leading, always with no disturbance of the children's sense of freedom. Child-centred psychodrama operates with spontaneity as the key to the whole process, but it does not follow the path of totally free play. It also clearly diverges from Melanie Klein's Freudian-based play therapy with its strong emphasis on psychoanalytic interpretations (Klein 1932). The insights gained by the child are, no doubt, linked to the hidden world of earlier developmental phases, but this form of therapy does not attempt to uncover such links explicitly.

To understand what it does seek to do, we need to sharpen the focus of terms used somewhat loosely in this book up until now. What is psychodrama? What makes it so powerful? And what exactly are the 'methods' and 'interventions' mentioned in previous pages? In order to find the answers to these questions, we need to grapple with the obscurities of Moreno's own writing, and to see psychodrama against the background of his theory of child development. A certain discipline of mind is required as we do this. But the task is worth the effort. It will shed a stronger light on the children's stories by the time we reach them. We will understand more fully the impact of their play, and we will see more clearly the therapist's role as healer and provocateur within the context of that play.

2

SPONTANEITY – THE LINCHPIN OF PSYCHODRAMA

> More important than science is its result.
> One answer provokes a hundred questions.
> (Moreno)

Ever since Freud presented his ground-breaking psycho-analytic theory of human development, the frontiers of understanding have been pushed further and further. The object of study is not something tangible and physically measurable, so the theories that have been advanced remain open to argument, and argument does indeed continue.

Moreno, writing as early as 1944, had long been dissatisfied with what Daniel Stern (1985) calls the 'working backward in time' approaches of early psycho-analytical theorists. He expressed his thought in similar language: 'The psycho-analytic investigator pushes backwards towards the trauma. The pyschodramatist pushes forward towards the act' (Moreno and Moreno 1944:44).

Marineau (1989) comments: 'He was more interested in the conscious process, the here and now, the creativity of the present, that the unconscious process, the past and the resistance of the "patient"' (Marineau 1989:31).

THE SPONTANEITY THEORY OF CHILD DEVELOPMENT

Well before 1944, Moreno had developed the highly complex action-based systems of psychodrama and sociodrama, centred around a new working hypothesis as to the primary forces affecting early childhood development. He stated: 'A hypothesis, covering the most mysterious part of human experience in its least articulate phase is here presented with reservation, awaiting consequent research to prove or disprove it' (Moreno and Moreno 1944:41).

His theories were startlingly different from those of his contemporaries. In their written form, he expressed them in new and unconventional language that was often difficult to follow. But it was the sheer unexpectedness of his central concepts that proved the greatest obstacle for many.

He postulated the existence of a spontaneity factor at the centre of an infant's earliest functioning; and he saw even the pre-natal child as being an active co-operator with the mother as it moved towards the moment of birth. He viewed birth, not as a trauma, but as a 'deep-reaching catharsis for the mother as well as the infant' – an event for which they had prepared as partners for nine months. He spoke of the infant's superior 'act-hunger' causing it to seek a more stimulating and expanding environment outside the safety of the uterus at a much earlier stage of development than other animals. This was a completely new frame of reference for child development theory. Contrasting it with the psycho-analytic viewpoint, Moreno claimed:

> A spontaneity theory of child development evaluates the growth of the infant in positive terms, and in terms of progression, rather than in negative terms and in terms of retardation and regression.
>
> (Moreno 1946:67)

This concept of a 'spontaneity factor' demands some unravelling. Before turning our minds to such a task, however, it is useful to side-track a little and to look at some of the evidence from modern research that fascinatingly extends our understanding of the new-born human infant's active engagement with life. Berg and Berg (1979) identify 'interest' as a human emotion evident at birth, with the infant continuing to respond to changes in stimulus intensity and complexity as it develops. Friedrich (1983) quotes Lewis Lipsitt (Director of the Child Study Centre at Brown University):

> The human infant is extremely well co-ordinated and put together for accomplishing the tasks of infancy. These are: sustenance, maintaining contact with other people, and defending itself against noxious stimulation.

There are studies that demonstrate these three functions occurring very soon after birth (e.g. infants only twelve hours old show aversion to noxious substances). In other studies, MacKain *et al.* (1981) and Kuhl and Meltzoff (1982) found (in separate experiments) that infants could recognize the connection between visual images and sound. They presented the infants with faces seen simultaneously and articulating different sounds. When only one of these sounds could be heard by the infants, they turned their attention to the face articulating that sound. They linked the sound with the movement of the mouth. Field *et al.* (1982) reported that infants as young as two days old would imitate an adult's frowns, smiles or facial expressions of surprise.

Most significant of all, Meltzoff and Moore (1977) demonstrated that babies only twelve days old would imitate adults sticking out a tongue. This indicated an ability to combine the brain's perception of two different activities (in this case, vision and muscular action). Psychologists see this ability as an essential first step in the process of thinking.

In his book *The Interpersonal World of the Infant*, Daniel Stern (1985) gives a more detailed and analytical review of many such studies that reveal what babies know. He addresses several complex issues arising out of them, and postulates the existence of an as yet unidentified 'innate general capacity' (transcending the sensory modes with which we are familiar) which allows the infant to process information in a 'supra-modal form'.

> It is not, then, a simple issue of a direct translation across modalities. Rather, it involves an encoding into a still mysterious amodal *representation*, which can then be recognized in any of the sensory modes.
>
> (Stern 1985:51)

The research question for the future, says Stern, is: *how* do infants know what they know?

In an earlier period, Moreno had continued to pursue his observations, without the benefits computers bring to research, but with all the benefits of a mind prepared to examine familiar data in totally new ways. Let us now return to his thinking, and follow through the connections with the pyschodramatic methods he had been concurrently developing for many years as a therapist.

Moreno observed that the infant:

needs aides in order to eat, sleep or move around in space. From the point of view of the child, these helpers appear like extensions to his own body, as he is too weak and immature to produce these actions by his own efforts.

(Moreno 1946:581)

Moreno called these assisting adults 'auxiliary egos'. The infant's growing interaction with them (as he slowly developed his sense of identity) was seen in terms of a series of roles and role reversals – a concept interestingly in tune with the modern research quoted above (Field *et al.* 1982; and Meltzoff and Moore 1977).

Observing the infant's lengthy period of dependency, Moreno described it as:

an eager apprenticeship, progressing, maturing and graduating into a world which is incomparably more complicated than the world into which the primate infant graduates, and for whose successful integration he needs incomparably greater resourcefulness (the *s* factor).

(Moreno 1946:67)

It is time we examined this *s* factor more closely. What is it? And what does Moreno mean by 'spontaneity'? Of the *s* factor, he says:

There must be a factor with which Nature has graciously provided the newcomer, so that he can land safely and anchor himself, at least provisionally, on an uncharted universe. This factor is more than and different from the given energy conserved in the body of the newborn. It is a factor which enables him to reach beyond himself, to enter new situations as if carrying the organism, stimulating, and arousing all its organs to modify their structures in order that they can meet their new responsibilities. To this factor, we apply the term spontaneity (*s* factor).

(*ibid*:50–51)

Spontaneity is difficult to define but this does not relieve us from asking what its meaning is.

(*ibid*:103)

Spontaneity, in Morenian terms, is true to its derivation from the Latin *sponte*, 'of free will'. It is:

a readiness of the subject to respond as required. It is a

condition – a conditioning – of the subject; a preparation of the subject for free action.

(ibid: 111–112)

If this statement applies to an infant at the moment of birth, or in the early post-natal period of its life when cognition and decision-making are not present in any marked degree, Cooke (1996) would take issue with Moreno here. Her research (1978) clearly distinguishes between 'response' and 'reaction'. Response, in her terms, involves cognition and decision-making. She would see the infant as merely 'reacting' (Cooke 1996:43–45). But Moreno's language and his manner of pursuing an argument lack the disciplined precision of a clinical psychologist's thought, and it is not always possible to pin down his concepts with satisfying clarity in their written form. To me, his written statements are far less compelling than the powerful therapeutic methods he developed in practice.

I am reminded here of Stern's comments on his own much later work:

The value of this working theory remains to be proved, and even its status as a hypothesis remains to be explored. Is it to be taken as a scientific hypothesis that can be evaluated by its confirming or invalidating current propositions, and by spawning studies that lead elsewhere? Or is it to be taken as a clinical metaphor to be used in practice, in which case the therapeutic efficacy of the metaphor can be determined?

(Stern 1985:275)

Moreno's genius lies in the 'therapeutic efficacy' of psychodrama, rather than in the creation of an hypothesis that could be tested scientifically. During my training, I experienced the efficacy of what Stern calls 'a clinical metaphor'. We worked, not from weighty, abstruse tomes, but through the texts of each other's lives. And it was from there that I discovered the transforming potency of psychodrama. That is why I began to use it with children.

There is, however, value in staying a little longer with Moreno's written description of the thinking behind psychodrama. He has more to say about the central significance of spontaneity and creativity, and about the primordial and universal nature of action-therapy.

14

In the context of his theory of child development and within the framework of psychodrama, Moreno and Moreno (1944:46) define spontaneity as a new and adequate response to a new situation or new response to an old situation. He later continues:

> the response to a novel situation requires a sense of timing, an imagination for appropriateness, an originality of self-propelling in emergencies, for which a special function is responsible.
>
> (Moreno 1946:93)

Moreno believed the human infant needed such a function. It is confronted by an extraordinary array of new situations. Equally extraordinary is the ability of the individual to respond, with no previous experience or model to guide it. It may well be that a particular response fits into categories that observers of children have formed over the years. It may be seen by these observers as predictable, to some degree. But for the individual infant, it is a triumphant and uniquely creative use of power when faced with the unexpected and the new. The s factor is in operation.

Moreno saw spontaneity as going beyond what genes and social forces determine and as being a factor that was as capable of measurement and examination as were intelligence, memory, association, etc. (Moreno and Moreno 1944:44). He postulated that spontaneity and creativity should be regarded as *'primary* and *positive* phenomena, and not as derivatives of libido or any other animal drive' (*ibid*:7).

Like all theories, this one simply represents a particular way of organizing existing knowledge. And like all theories, it provides a particular pathway for seeking new knowledge. The path followed determines what will be found. Psychodrama, in its classical form, developed as Moreno explored this path. He knew that his central hypothesis might well be disproved by future gene technology, but he chose to pursue his testing of it, saying:

> It seems to be more stimulating to the present state of bio-genetic and social research to assume that there is within the range of individual expression an independent area between heredity and environment ... an area from which human inventiveness and creativity merges [i.e. his s factor].

15

The *s* factor is the soil out of which later the spontaneous, creative matrix of personality grows.

(Moreno 1946:51)

It is beyond my charter to attempt a summary of Moreno's prolific writings on this subject, interesting though that might be. For it is important not to allow the children's voices (which are so central to this book) to be swamped by convoluted arguments and elaborate theoretical discussion. However, it could be valuable, and even necessary, at this point briefly to outline those features of the psychodramatic method that predominantly influenced my work with these children.

PSYCHODRAMA

Building on his theories of the central importance of spontaneity and creativity, and of the primordial significance of 'the act', Moreno describes five instruments of the psychodramatic method:

1 The stage
2 The protagonist
3 The director
4 The auxiliary egos
5 The audience

The stage   (as conceptualized by Moreno) is a multi-layered space, circular in shape, able to be used metaphorically (for example, to indicate levels of aspiration, dimensions of time, etc.).

The protagonist   is asked to be himself on the stage, to portray *his own private world*. 'He has to act freely, as things rise up in his mind; that is why he has to be given freedom of expression, spontaneity' (Moreno 1946).

The protagonist explores a personal issue. A relationship of trust must exist between him and the director if the enactment is to have therapeutic depth.

The director   uses many techniques to assist the protagonist to warm up to the process that comes next in importance to spontaneity – the enactment. These techniques include scene-setting,

16

the use of doubling, mirroring, maximizing, concretizing, and a challenging use of auxiliary egos.

These terms, as used in my adaptation of psychodrama for children, are defined as follows:

Doubling involves moving alongside the protagonist, reproducing the movements and words and becoming as fully in tune as possible with the unexpressed inner state. (In my work, I sometimes extend this to doubling for the puppet, in its role as auxiliary, rather than for the protagonist.)

Mirroring enables the director to reflect back to the protagonist a mood, a style of speech, or a way of acting that has just been displayed.

Concretizing moves the exploration of a situation away from mere words. It includes physical actions and, in my work, the use of puppets and dolls to create pictures and enliven the child's words, accentuating the experience of play.

Maximizing occurs when the director helps the protagonist to magnify and expand an idea, or mood, or reaction in a dramatic form.

Scene-setting involves the creation of a three-dimensional picture, using the puppets, as the child relates an event. The director causes this to happen with commands such as 'Choose something to be X', or 'Where is the train? Make something be the train'. With older children, it is sometimes necessary to assist in creating the atmosphere surrounding the scene, for example: 'So, you're rocking in the train with your mates – talking, laughing, smoking', but younger children rarely need this. Their own play has the power to draw them right in to the atmosphere of the scenes they spontaneously create, and at once action follows.

The director often introduces an element of surprise into the enactment (e.g. suddenly directing the protagonist to reverse roles with the auxiliary ego – a person who may be acting for him in the role of a character in the scene he is creating – or who may be portraying another aspect of the protagonist's own character). This surprises the protagonist into facing an unexpected new situation. He is forced to be spontaneous (or to freeze into inaction). Out of this, new insights come, with far more power than they would if he were left to himself, merely re-enacting a known incident or portraying one out of his existing imagination. The spontaneity–creativity factor comes into play.

The auxiliary egos are actors who represent absentee persons as they appear in the private world of the [protagonist] (Moreno 1946:xviii). In classical psychodrama, the protagonist chooses them from among members of the group. In my work, the puppets take the place of group members. As indicated above, the auxiliary egos take a very active role in assisting the protagonist's exploration of himself and of his life. They work *for the protagonist* and also *for the director.*

The audience in psychodrama has a double purpose:

1 To be a sounding board of public opinion for the protagonist, making spontaneous responses and comments or sometimes responding with cheers, laughter, sounds of protest, etc. (but always within a context of acceptance of the protagonist, and with respect for the therapeutic process).
2 The members of the audience may be helped by all that they see portrayed in the enactment.

Moreno emphasizes the importance of the active involvement of the auxiliary egos and the audience.

> The protagonist in a psychodrama is never as alone as the nocturnal dreamer. Without the counterforces which the auxiliary egos and the members of the group inject, the opportunities for the protagonist to learn would be very much reduced.
>
> (Moreno 1946:xv)

Whenever the director uses one of the many techniques Moreno devised, the aim is

> not to turn the [protagonists] into actors, but rather to stir them up to be on stage what they ARE, more deeply than they appear to be in life reality.
>
> (*ibid*:c)

To what effect? Moreno replies: 'Catharsis' (*ibid*:d).

Because psychodrama centres on *the act* (which is universal and primordial in nature), it transcends the barriers of language. The protagonist is constantly moving forward to the unpredictable, opening the way for spontaneity. Body and mind are engaged together and feeling is tapped at unexpectedly deep levels. The resulting catharsis is far more than the release of emotion. Moreno calls it 'mental catharsis', a term that he borrows from Aristotle. He sees a cathartic experience that is enacted as being superior to one that involves mere listening and watching. 'It is into the stream of action catharsis that the rivulets of partial catharsis flow' (*ibid*:18).

Action-therapy is a medium that fits naturally into the world of children. Role-play and role-reversal have been part of life for them since infancy. Spontaneity is still frequently operative in their lives. The demarcation between fantasy and reality is less rigid for them than it is for most adults, and they can move flexibly from one to another. Their words are not sufficient to express all that they know, all that they experience:

> The methods of interview, indeed all verbal semantics, are only rarely fully effective in the adjustment of the problems of the child and the adolescent. The relief coming from interview has to be replaced by the catharsis of action, working out their problems as their own actors on the stage, or by spectator catharsis with a staff of auxiliary egos mirroring the problems which [they] have by means of dramatic presentation.
>
> (*ibid*:145)

This is the natural medium for children. All the above intellectualizing discussion has no place in their lives. As they weave in and out of the reality and fantasy that form the stuff of their play, they have a freedom that adults envy. Their spontaneity leads to insights that are deep and life-changing. The adult who seeks to enter that play in the role of therapist must do so with knowledge, care and precision, and with total acceptance of the child.

Photo: Linda Gallus

3

THE WAY IN

A meeting of two : eye to eye, face to face,
And when you are near I will tear your eyes out
and place them in place of mine
. . .
then I will look at you with your eyes.
(Moreno)

The previous chapters dealt with the theoretical and philo-sophical framework behind this way of working. Now the focus will be sharpened in an attempt to answer the question often asked by therapists wishing to explore this method: 'How does one begin?' The following steps form the base plan in the intro-ductory stages of working with any child, but from the moment of meeting the child there is no predicting the path that will open out.

INTRODUCTORY STEPS

Interview with parents or significant adults in the child's daily life. The main purpose of this interview has two components: firstly, to allow the parents to clarify their reasons for seeking therapy for the child and, at the same time, to assess their degree of comfort in working with this particular therapist; secondly, to give the therapist background information that is accessible only via the parents or care-givers. This provides a view of the child through their eyes, and reveals many of the parents' values and the roles they habitually act out. The child's self-image may later emerge as quite different. But the therapist's task of learning to look out on the world through the child's eyes has begun. Some very tentative hypotheses can begin to form in response to the unspoken question: 'What might it be like to be this child in this particular family, with its own particular structure, its own particular values?'

Very occasionally, in families with a black-and-white view of human behaviour, that structure and those values are so different from the therapist's approach to children that joint work cannot be undertaken. Sometimes the parents decide to terminate the therapy, even in spite of signs of obvious progress. But where there is compatibility between the parents' wishes and the therapist's goals, this first interview is invaluable to all who take part in it. It forms the basis of an ongoing working partnership.

To the parents, the therapist makes it clear that the insights they have gained through years of living with the child have a value of their own, and they will not be ignored. Equally important, their desires, hopes or fears regarding the therapy itself will also not be swept aside. They are given time to ask questions about the methods that will be used. The delicate issue of trust and confidentiality is given a full airing. The therapist cannot reach a disturbed child if the parents require every detail of the session to be revealed to them; but neither can the parents co-operate with the therapy if they are told nothing. The balance that needs to be struck varies from family to family. But whatever the form this balance takes, it is never allowed to interfere with the child's ability to be free in a therapy session, and to know that trust will never be betrayed. (In practice, I have never found it difficult to obtain a child's permission to reveal important material to parents when the need for this arises. But the revealing is done with the child's knowledge, and often in a joint session with the relevant family members.)

> The therapist needs to approach this first session (and, indeed, all others) with an awareness of the background presence of the past – for the therapist, as well as for the child and the parents, the phenomena of transference and counter-transference can come into play, with 'expectations, fears and problems transferred from the past'.
>
> (Salzberger-Wittenberg 1970:17)

This has important implications for the ongoing therapy, so we shall interrupt this step-by-step discussion for a moment to consider what could be called the wild card in the pack – counter-transference.

Therapists are often aware of clients bringing earlier repressed fears, conflicts and longings into the therapeutic relationship, but they sometimes are less ready to see how their own ancient memories can stir irrational responses to events that occur in the course of therapy. Mannoni (1967) reminds us that every time one confronts a child in a clinical setting

> the analyst is faced with his own representation of childhood, and the weight of his unconscious motivation will make itself felt in the manner in which he handles the treatment. The child and his family arouse the most primitive fears, defences and anxiety in the analyst – he is always being forced into the field where everyone is brought face-to-face with the problem of desire, death and the Law.
>
> (Mannoni 1967:14)

When one is working with the parents of highly disturbed children, such self-awareness is often needed, alongside a quite pragmatic understanding of the normalcy of the frustrations they may express – frustrations connected with the constant day-to-day living with a disturbed child; with the slowness of change; with the insulated 'otherness' of the therapy setting. But these are considerations that usually belong a little further down the road. Let us return in time to the first interview.

The final purpose of this session is to work out with the parents the best way for them to invite the child to come. This involves assisting the parents to find the right words to express truthfully to the child the reason for their seeking help. The reason usually includes some needs of the parents as well as those of the child, but often it does not occur to them to state this. By putting the whole focus on the child, they imply blame or weakness which can be bitterly resented and resisted. This conversation with the child also needs to include some idea of the therapist's use of play with children who've had some difficult experiences or who are feeling unhappy or confused. We work out the words that will best convey this. The child's warm-up to the whole therapeutic process is assisted (or dampened) by the parents' way of broaching the subject.

REFLECTIONS ON WHAT HAS EMERGED

The approach in this way of working has little in common with pathology-conscious theories. So the reflective process that now follows is not a meticulous sifting of data, aimed at producing a psycho-social history, complete with diagnosis and treatment plans. At this stage there is instead a somewhat contemplative openness to all that has been presented, verbally and non-verbally, during the two-way interaction in the first meeting between parents and therapist. In that session, the therapist was often in a learning role, with antennae tuned to pick up anything that would assist an entry into the child's inner world. What is needed now is the creation of a gentle, meditative space where new insights will have a chance to surface. I live by the sea, so for me this reflecting is usually done as I walk on the beach. The wide expanse of the sea and the sand's quick response to my footsteps are for me very evocative symbols. They express my desire to be open to all I can learn in my work with this child. The work has begun before we have even met.

Now, as the insights from that preliminary interview are allowed to shift, or settle, or surface, the focus is on forming a tentative hypothesis as to what might be at the heart of the problem *for the child*. The adults who made the referral have put their view of it, but the therapist's major task is to discover the child's perception. This tentative hypothesis might well need to be discarded (perhaps as early as the first session). But, in making one, the therapist has already come to terms with the need to respect the child's own experience as the starting point for therapy – and also, no doubt, with the difficulties of the task. So many years of living separate the worlds of child and therapist. It is easy to assume that facts which seem obvious to adults are also obvious to children; or that the insights of childhood (clear-eyed and precise) are equally available to adults, encumbered as we are by the luggage of the years.

THE FIRST SESSION

Before the child arrives, the therapist needs to take a little time to get in touch with 'the child within'. For me, that includes opening my mind to meeting an enjoyable playmate, in much the same way as I had observed relaxed, confident children doing on entering a birthday party room when I was a child. Back in those far-off days, I was more likely to be diffident and a little nervous of my approval rating. But today, I can access an inner freedom that allows me to greet this child in openness. I am confident the next hour will be delightful. I offer what I am, and I greet the child as an equal.

'Hullo', I say, after I open the door, and I look at the child with the interest and pleasure I feel in beginning this new encounter. Then I smile at the parent, as one greets a friend already known, inviting them both to come in. Invariably, the child looks back at me with answering directness (sometimes shyly and cautiously, sometimes with alert eagerness), and the reply is always: 'Hullo'. From the beginning, the child experiences our equality, and from the opening moments of the session, parent and child are afforded equal respect. Many children we see as therapists are aware of adults as potentially condescending authority figures, before whom they have been landed because someone has decided they need to be 'fixed'. A mixture of resentment and fear can cause them to activate their impenetrable defence mechanisms if this perception remains. An atmosphere of anxiety pervades, and spontaneity is impossible.

But if parents and therapist have worked together with understanding, the child comes to the first session with only the usual caution that encounters with strangers demands. The session is structured to allow the child time to observe this new person at leisure, beginning with a brief resumé of the purpose of the visit, followed by a low-key exploration of the puppets, and then a free-play session. With some children, there can be a total by-passing of this undemanding exploratory play. They seem to have come to this meeting with the unknown therapist having a sense of purpose of their own. Their body language expresses this as I meet them at the door or as they engage with me in those first few moments of relaxing conversation. It tells me they have what Winnicott (1971) describes as 'a sense of occasion'. There is a look of hope in their eyes that the person in front of them has special importance in this troubled period of their lives. Speaking of the significance of the first interview, Winnicott describes these initial encounters as

special occasions that have a quality that has made me use the word sacred. Either this sacred moment is used or it is

25

wasted. If it is wasted the child's belief in being understood is shattered. If, on the other hand, it is used, then the child's belief in being helped is strengthened. There will be those cases in which deep work is done in the special circumstances of the first interview (or interviews) and the resulting changes in the child can be made use of by parents and those responsible in the immediate social setting, so that whereas a child was caught up in a knot in regard to the emotional development, the interview has resulted in a loosening of the knot and a forward movement in the developmental process.

(Winnicott 1971:4–5)

The reader will see a similar progression occurring for several of the children whose stories appear later in this book.

For many children, however, the first session reveals, on the surface, little more than their preferred ways of playing and perhaps some hints of the metaphorical significance of particular puppets for them. Klein (1932) describes the value of this to the observant therapist.

we shall have got some idea of its unconscious on which to base our analytic work from having noticed what sort of game it has started, at what point its resistance has set in [if this occurs], how it has behaved in connection with that resistance, what chance remark it may have dropped at the time and so on.

(Klein 1932:33)

But let us never forget that just as the therapist is observing the child, so too the child is summing up the therapist. No matter how absorbing the play, and no matter how well concealed is this covert activity, we can be certain it does occur. And the child's observations are likely to be highly accurate. The relationship-centred therapy that follows is strongly influenced by this first session. My collection of toys, puppets and play materials is quite extensive. It includes human characters and animals from many different countries – squirrels, a mole, a skunk, a raccoon, lions, tigers, elephants. Because I work in Australia, the children are often drawn to the familiar and well-loved animals that are native to this country. No doubt, therapists in other lands see children drawn to what is loved and familiar to them. It is important to follow their attraction. This is often revealed in the first session.

Psychodrama-based child therapy is a form of therapy suffused with metaphor. The therapist who works in this way must be open to a language that

> implies something more than its obvious and immediate meaning. It has a wider 'unconscious' aspect that is never precisely defined or fully explained. Nor can one hope to define or explain it. As the mind explores the symbol, it is led to ideas that lie beyond the grasp of reason.
>
> (Jung 1964:20–21)

This chapter, with its emphasis on cognition and analysis, leads on to the free-wheeling world of the children's therapeutic play. As we leave ponderous theoretical considerations behind, we need to move closer to that part of ourselves that responds to imagery and ambiguity, or we shall not be able to follow where the children lead. Let us spend a little time allowing this to happen.

Photo: Margaret Sail

4

METAPHOR, ARCHETYPE AND STORY – THE HIDDEN LANGUAGE

Tread softly because you tread on my dreams
(W. B. Yeats, 'He Wishes for the Cloths of Heaven')

Long ago, I came upon a book that delighted my mind and spoke to depths of my being that elude analysis. It was Sam Keen's *Apology for Wonder*. It is suddenly invading my mind again as I turn to consider the extraordinary freedom with which some children create healing metaphors in their play. Keen uses the imagery of two very different gods, Apollo and Dionysus, to compare two very different models that typify modern man. His descriptions of the Apollonian way of living fit the life-style of many modern Westerners. Logic, pragmatism, and order predominate. 'Man shares with the gods the responsibility for creating a cosmos in which reason and order prevail. The rule of law is the path of wisdom' (Keen 1969:153). But there is another way of living. It has its own imagery.

> Dionysus was a strange and wild god ... [and] the model for the Dionysian way is the dance. Life is flux, movement, a dynamic power which assumes form for a moment and then changes. There is no end point, no complete product.
>
> (Keen 1969:156)

And that is the world these children know when, in play, they leap from insight to insight, not bothering to fill in all the rational sequential steps as they go. 'Wisdom in the Dionysian tradition consists of continuing openness to the diverse and sometimes contradictory streams that flow through the depths of man.' (*ibid*:155). The children are not concerned about contradictions, unless some adult is trying to pin them down to explain, in logical sentences, the maelstrom of half-experienced thoughts and emotions that sometimes flood their consciousness. In play, there is no need to explain. With their imaginations stimulated by the puppets, they are open to a world of metaphor and symbolism that leads them forward with a force of its own.

I came upon Mills and Crowley's (1986) interesting exploration of therapeutic metaphors quite some time after I had set off on my own journey of discovery. The children had already surprised me by their ability to engage so profoundly with their problems through psychodrama-enhanced play. 'What gives it such power?' was a question that often tugged at my mind. I already knew that psychodrama's spontaneity-centred, action-based techniques had an ability to cut through intellectualizing defences, bringing hidden material suddenly to the surface. But it was only when I read Mills and Crowley's review of the literature, linking metaphor with the functioning of the right brain, that I realized how deeply psychodrama techniques tap into a child's natural affinity with metaphor. And I gained a more physiologically orientated understanding of the connection between metaphor and the emotions, and metaphor and psychosomatic symptoms. Let us take time to focus on some of the concepts Mills and Crowley develop in so much more detail in their study of metaphor.

Their book shows the influence of Milton Erickson, whose extraordinary skills with metaphor began to develop as he searched for ways of coping with disabling illness of his own as a young boy. Later, he told clients stories that contained what his colleague, Rossi, called 'two-level communication' – a means of communicating with both the conscious and unconscious minds. Mills and Crowley summarize as follows:

> When the conscious mind is provided with one message (in the form of concepts, ideas, stories, images) which keeps it 'occupied', another therapeutic message can be slipped to the unconscious mind via implication and connotation. . . . While the conscious mind is listening to the literal aspects of the anecdote, the carefully designed, interspersed suggestions are activating unconscious associations and shifting meanings which accumulate and finally 'spill over' into consciousness.
>
> (Mills and Crowley 1986:18)

They go on to quote Erickson and Rossi, developing the idea:

> The conscious mind is surprised because it is presented with a response within itself that it cannot account for. . . . Analogy and metaphor as well as jokes can be understood as exerting their powerful effects through the same mechanisms of activating unconscious association patterns and response tendencies that suddenly summate to present consciousness with an apparently 'new' datum of behavioural response.
>
> (Erickson and Rossi 1976:448)

(This was an interesting description of the process that appeared to be in place in the therapeutic storytelling and metaphor-laden psychodrama sessions with the children that were already part of my work.)

Mills and Crowley then move on to review the studies of the 1960s and 1970s, when considerable progress was made in analysing the separate functions of the right and left hemispheres of the brain. They quote the work of Luria (1973) and Galin (1974) who found that the right hemisphere was more involved than the left in mediating *emotional and imagistic processes* (Mills and Crowley 1986:17) and link these findings with later studies that indicate a connection with metaphor.

According to Mills and Crowley, Nebes (1977) found that 'the left brain processes language sequentially, logically and literally, while the right brain processes it in a simultaneous, holistic and implicative fashion', and Ornstein (1978) pursued the implications of this for metaphor, in a study that compared brain-wave activity during the reading of technical passages with that during the reading of Sufi stories. 'The Sufi stories produced the same left hemisphere activity as the technical *plus* a surge of involvement in the right hemisphere', suggesting that the right hemispheric involvement was required for *processing the metaphor* and discovering the meaning of the story. Rogers *et al.*'s earlier (1977) work also had implications for metaphor. It demonstrated the presence of higher right brain activity when a story was being processed in a language that is more contextual than English – that is, a language in which words do not have fixed meanings, depending on their context for their interpretation. This is how metaphor functions.

These separate findings interested me, not in terms of the

newness of the ideas, but rather through the way in which they can be linked with Erickson and Rossi's suggestion that their use of 'mythopoetic language may thus be a means of communicating directly with the right hemisphere in its own language' (Erickson and Rossi 1979:144). They suggested that the use of metaphorical approaches to therapy accounts for its being less time-consuming than psycho-analytically orientated approaches.

> This [use of metaphorical language to communicate directly with the right hemisphere] is in contrast to the conventional psychoanalytic approach of first translating the right hemisphere's body language into the abstract patterns of cognition of the left hemisphere, which must somehow operate back upon the right hemisphere to change the symptom.
> (Erickson and Rossi 1979:144)

Mills and Crowley sum it up: 'Metaphor, on the other hand, goes straight for the target area – the right brain process' (Mills and Crowley 1986:17–18).

How does all this fit with the world of children? Classical psychodrama involves a high level of right brain activity, with the director constantly taking the protagonist into the realm of the imagination and continually calling for spontaneous reactions to the unexpected. Because of children's greater openness to fantasy and metaphor, the adaptation of psychodrama described in this book involves even higher levels of right brain activity for them than for most adults. This activity is reflected in the labile, imagistic play of the children, in the metaphor-charged therapeutic stories, and in the intrinsic power of the puppets and toys to evoke multiple associations.

Jung would doubtless also note the archetypal nature of many of the symbols used, and he would claim that this provides an added pathway to the unconscious mind.

> Archetypes are inherited elements of the human psyche which reflect common patterns of experience throughout the history of human consciousness. Another way to say this would be to say that archetypes are *metaphorical prototypes* representing the many milestones in mankind's evolution. There are the mother and father archetypes, the masculine and feminine archetypes, the child archetypes, and so on. For Jung the archetypes were 'living psychic forces' as

real as our physical bodies. The archetypes were to the spirit what our organs are to the body.

(Mills and Crowley 1986:13)

Neither the children nor I deliberately stop, in the course of imaginative play or in the creating of a therapeutic story, to search for an image that would tap into what Jung calls 'the collective unconscious'. He defines it as that deeper layer of the unconscious

> that does not derive from personal experience, and is not a personal acquisition but is inborn. This deeper layer I call the *collective unconscious.* I have chosen the term 'collective' because this part of the unconscious is not individual but universal; in contrast to the personal psyche, it has contents and modes of behaviour that are more or less the same everywhere and in all individuals. It is, in other words, identical in all men and this constitutes a common psychic substrate of a suprapersonal nature which is present in every one of us.
>
> (Jung 1934:3–4)

But time and time again we did use images that Jung lists as having archetypal significance – images that were expressed in many forms, in ancient myths and fairy tales. The references to nature in many of my stories are an example of this. They had an impact that went far beyond their power to evoke memories of familiar scenes.

> All the mythologized processes of nature, such as summer and winter, the phases of the moon, the rainy seasons and so forth, are in no sense allegories of these objective occurrences; rather they are symbolic expressions of the inner, unconscious drama of the psyche which becomes accessible to man's consciousness by way of projection – that is, mirrored in the events of nature.
>
> (*ibid*:6)

With one child in particular this choice of imagery (based on his own interests and the form of communicating that had grown between us) had deeper implications of which I was not conscious at the time. Following hints from the child's play, I began a series of stories involving the moon (a mother symbol in Jungian

33

thinking) and the sea (symbol for 'the unconscious, the mother of all that lives' (*ibid*:178)). They were apt symbols for the work involved in helping this child release the effects of trauma, and went far beyond his own love of the sea, and his interest in nature.

Jung's elaboration of the child archetype throws interesting additional light on any child therapy work.

> The motif of 'smaller than small yet bigger than big' complements the impotence of the child by means of its equally miraculous deeds. This paradox is the essence of the hero and runs through his whole destiny like a red thread. He can cope with the greatest perils, yet, in the end something quite insignificant is his undoing.
>
> (*ibid*:167)

Very often a therapist's task involves helping the child to identify and deal with 'something quite insignificant' and dealing with it leads to 'miraculous deeds' on the part of the child – insights that are sometimes astounding; action decisions that require courage; and so on. Jung's discussion of the 'collision of opposites' (when an individual is faced with 'an agonizing situation of conflict from which there seems to be no way out', *ibid*:167) also throws new light on the child's way of working through life dilemmas in play.

> But out of this collision of opposites the unconscious psyche always creates a third thing of an irrational nature, which the conscious mind neither expects nor understands. It presents itself in a form that is neither a straight 'yes' nor a straight 'no', and is consequently rejected by both. For the conscious mind knows nothing beyond the opposites and, as a result, has no knowledge of the thing that unites them.
>
> (*ibid*:167,168)

It is this very 'collision of opposites' and the search for 'the thing that unites them' that is addressed in psychodrama. Children do the searching through metaphor.

Therapeutic storytelling has been mentioned several times in this and preceding chapters. Jung is the great master of metaphor, and Erickson an exceptionally gifted exponent of its value in therapy, but Bettleheim is the most illuminating commentator on fairy tales. Many of his descriptions of fairy tales – how they are presented, why they are important, and why they work for children – equally apply to the form of therapeutic storytelling I have attempted to follow. Let us look at some of Bettleheim's lucidly expressed observations, and take what we can from them in relation to a child's needs and a therapist's goals.

> The more I tried to understand why these stories are so successful at enriching the inner life of the child, the more I realized that these tales, in a much deeper sense that any other reading material, *start where the child really is in his psychological and emotional being* [emphasis added]. They speak about his severe inner pressures in a way that the child unconsciously understands, and – without belittling the most serious struggles which growing up entails – offer examples of both temporary and permanent solutions to pressing difficulties.
>
> (Bettleheim 1976:6)

This is a very clear description of how a therapist must move when creating a healing story. It will only work for the child if it is presented from within the space that Bettleheim describes and in a form that leaves the child totally unpressured. The words, 'fairy tale' in the following quotation could well be replaced by 'therapeutic story' to extend this thought.

> The fairy tale is presented in a simple homely way; no demands are made on the listener. This prevents even the smallest child from feeling compelled to act in specific ways, and he is never made to feel inferior. Far from making demands, the fairy tale reassures, gives hope for the future and holds out the promise of a happy ending. That is why Lewis Carroll called it a 'love-gift'.
>
> (*ibid*:26)

For the therapist, many skills and much patience are involved in the creation of a healing story that makes no intrusions on the child's freedom. I remember waiting for months with one child before the right images would come to my mind. I knew she could best be reached through a story, but it had to be one that very precisely homed in to the heart of her problem. And it had to contain images that would work to free her without unduly challenging her defences. It was tempting to offer one that was *almost* right, for I was aware that she needed help. But it was necessary to wait. The story was left to germinate in my mind. I remember the evening it presented itself, with image after image – a fully fledged tale that would intrigue the child as a story in its own right, even while the metaphors worked below the surface. I was driving along a country road at the time, under an open sky lit with subtly changing pearl-like colour from the setting sun. It was just as well there was no other traffic, for I became quite excited as the story of Bellissima Splendoribus unfolded, and the world flew by for more than an hour. With other children, and less complex problems, stories come simply and more readily. Always, they involve a double process – a tapping in to one's diagnostic abilities as a therapist and a release of what Nancy Mellon believes is an innate gift.

> You, like every human being, are a storyteller by birthright. You are born with an endless supply of personal and universal themes. It is important to open yourself to receive the vast wealth of imagery that lives within you.
>
> (Mellon 1992:8)

Her encouraging and practical book, *Storytelling and the Art of the Imagination*, is not aimed at therapists, but it is very useful for anyone who wants to develop an untapped skill in storytelling.

Bettleheim, meanwhile, highlights other essential elements in the fairy tale's power to help a child to understand himself and to understand life.

> The dominant culture wishes to pretend, particularly where children are concerned, that the dark side of man does not exist, and professes a belief in an optimistic meliorism.
>
> (Bettleheim 1976:7,8)

The fairy tale indulges in no such shirking of reality. Good and evil meet, face to face – and the characters are drawn simplistically, without the ambivalence of real life. 'Evil is as omnipresent as virtue' (*ibid*:8).

> Presenting the polarities of character permits the child to comprehend easily the difference between the two, which he could not do as readily were the figures drawn more true to life, with all the complexities that characterize real people. Ambiguities must wait until a relatively firm

personality has been established on the basis of positive identifications.

(*ibid*: 9)

The therapeutic story also needs a clean-cut line, the figures clearly drawn, tension in the simple plot, and the therapeutic messages carefully interwoven in a story that excites the imagination. Above all, there must be no sermonizing. Better to have the life-enhancing messages so subtle that they are missed, than intrude on the child's imaginative world with a moralistic prescription for good living or even a single explanation. Students often ask me if I discuss the meaning of a story with the child who has just heard it. 'That would be like turning a hose on to a fire', I tell them. Bettleheim stresses the importance of not disturbing the connections that are going on within the child by superimposing an adult interpretation of a fairy tale, and the same holds true for a therapeutic story.

> Explaining to a child why a fairy tale is so captivating to him destroys, moreover, the story's enchantment, which depends to a considerable degree on the child's not quite knowing why he is delighted by it. And with the forfeiture of this power to enchant goes also a loss of the story's potential for helping the child struggle on his own, and master all by himself the problem which has made the story meaningful to him in the first place. Adult interpretations, as correct as they may be, rob the child of the opportunity to feel that he, on his own, through repeated hearing and ruminating about the story, has coped successfully with a difficult situation.

> (*ibid*:18,19)

In the case of therapeutic storytelling, there are added, and very important, reasons why the therapist should not explain the symbolism. If the child's defence mechanisms need to remain in place, and the therapist has made a mistake in timing (or, for that matter, in interpretation), the child enjoys the story for its own sake and the inner meaning is undetected. If the therapist tries to force the pace of healing, the force will be met by discomfort, confusion and resistance. A far more important process, to which children are more open than adults, will be insensitively disturbed. Bettleheim describes it with characteristic lucidity:

In order to master the psychological problems of growing up . . . a child needs to understand what is going on within his conscious self so that he can also cope with what goes on in his unconscious. He can achieve this understanding, and with it the ability to cope, not through rational comprehension of the nature and content of his unconscious, but by becoming familiar with it through spinning out daydreams – ruminating, re-arranging, and fantasizing about suitable story elements in response to unconscious pressures. By doing this, the child fits unconscious content into conscious fantasies, which then enable him to deal with that content.

(*ibid*:7)

A similar process goes on in play. When this play is extended and further energized by Moreno's methods, the images gain new power. The children go on to make life-enhancing connections, often at quite unexpected depths, but in the silence of their own minds.

Jung describes the transformation that ensues:

When there is merely the image, then there is simply a word picture of little consequence. But by being charged with emotions, the image gains numinosity (or psychic energy); it becomes dynamic, and consequences of some kind must flow from it.

(Jung 1964:96)

I turn to the children for an illustration of this abstract thought. One child leaps to the forefront of my consciousness. She will remain nameless – a gesture of recognition of her need for privacy and control. We have known each other for some years now, and she has been one of my greatest teachers.

On this particular day, she had just been told her longed-for foster placement was not going ahead – in spite of several months of built-up hopes. In our play that day, she directed me to go to sleep on an improvised bed. Using a wig from our dressing-up collection, she turned it into a beard and said she was Father Christmas. She gave me many gifts, then told me to go back to sleep. While I was asleep, she literally stripped the therapy room of everything moveable (toys, books, chairs, small tables), leaving only a heavy desk and an empty book-case. As I lay there with my eyes shut, I felt the vibrations of her ferociously energetic footsteps, and I heard the sound of the next room being filled with objects she was dragging from the therapy room. Using Moreno's doubling principles, I internally identified with the urgency and violence of her emotion. When she allowed me to open my eyes, I experienced the full impact of the denuded room.

If I had not known about the ditched foster-care plans (and, at this stage of her therapy, she would never have told me herself), I would not have been able to interpret the metaphor as fully as I succeeded in doing. The notion of deprivation was obvious, of course, and of trust betrayed. Without background knowledge, I probably would have been able to respond in play to these. But I certainly would have missed the true depth of her anguish and rage for, characteristically, she had set the game up as full of laughter as well. By maximizing the sense of desolation as I played the role of the child, I was able to trigger her spontaneity further. Our play led to her spontaneously making some real-life comments before she left (a first for her). They included an explicit expression of her anger and desolation at her mother's perceived abandonment of her. She had never acknowledged such emotions before. She followed this up with an unusual action-decision of her own that obviously arose out of her later reflections on the session (another first). Years down the track, she has by now lost much of her Dionysian flair, and no longer explodes into brilliant metaphor when faced with life's crises. She is still very wary of revealing herself through words, so it is more difficult to help her find healing.

It would be possible to work with children using only the knowledge they present so obliquely, and having no background information. But the therapeutic process would then require a much longer time-frame, such as that used by Virginia Axline (1964) in her delicate, patient work with Dibs. In my work, I rarely have the luxury of unlimited time. The children's lives move on, imposing new pressures, demanding new perceptions; and the parents, too, often find that their ability to support ongoing therapy has its limits. However, when a therapist combines real-life knowledge with the alchemy of psychodrama, there is magic. The child's metaphorical play is lit from within, and new insights are facilitated with surprising speed. There is a surge of hope, which carries its own impetus for ongoing change. The child moves with it.

It is time now for us also to move – further away from the abstractions of theory and into the clear, unencumbered space each child created in the actual therapy sessions.

Part II

THE CHILDREN'S STORIES

In olden times, when wishing still helped,
there lived a king whose daughters were all beautiful,
but the youngest was so beautiful that the sun itself,
which has seen so much, was astonished
whenever it shone in her face.
                    (The Brothers Grimm: *The Frog King*)

Photo: Bernadette Hoey

5

ANDREA

Let us begin with Andrea's story. This twelve-year-old girl was in Year Six at a primary school where I often worked. Some months before I met her, her hair had begun to fall out in chunks and she had developed a habit of pulling it. There were now some bald patches on the side. On the top it had regrown like a spiky crewcut. The medical experts who had examined her believed that her condition (alopecia) was psychosomatic, hence my involvement.

My work with her was in line with fairly traditional psychodrama methods, and was not linked with therapeutic storytelling. I include it here, as it was the beginning of my use of puppets and dolls as auxiliaries. Andrea was mature enough to cope with direct role-reversal, but the younger children with whom I have worked could do this only very indirectly and through metaphor. Their ego boundaries were not sufficiently developed to allow them to step so fully into another person's shoes. For them, concepts such as doubling, mirroring, concretization were equally powerful tools for opening locked doors. However, in this account of that process they are hidden in the interactive play between child and therapist. They are therefore less clearly identifiable to readers unfamiliar with psychodrama. So Andrea's more explicit exploration of her problem provides a useful introduction to the fantasy-laden work of the younger children.

PRELIMINARY INTERVIEW

Aim: To introduce ourselves to each other and to work out the best time for a full session.

Andrea walks across with me from the school, apparently very relaxed. She is able to chat with ease and charm, maintaining the role of poised princess until I mention her problem. Then she cannot talk. Her eyes fill with tears. Her body language is that of a frightened child rather than the bright little pseudo-adult who has been relating to me. I comment on her unhappy, crumpled-up look, and the tears she is fighting back, and her wordlessness.

B. 'You're like someone else in this room.'
I move across to the chair where a large, almost life-size doll is curled up, her porcelain face half-hidden in the chair's cushion. I turn the doll's head around. Andrea can see a large tear painted on its cheek.
B. 'Do you know what she's crying about?'
Andrea shakes her head. I pull the scarf off the doll's head. It is as bald as an egg. The girl weeps silently, still fighting back the tears.
B. 'It's all right to cry in this room. People do it all the time. They need to let their tears out. So you can cry . . . I think you're feeling pretty scared.' [*A nods.*] 'Tell me about it.' [*A remains miserably wordless.*] 'Maybe I'll have to guess. . . . Maybe you're scared you could end up without any hair.' [*A nods.*] 'And kids can tease.' [*A nods. She looks relieved.*]
B. 'It's a pity we haven't more time today. There's a lot we could work on here. We've really just lifted a lid and had a quick look at what it's like. . . . When could you come back?'
We arrange a time on the following day, with a time-slot of at least an hour. Andrea leaves, looking relieved and happy.

POST-INTERVIEW REFLECTIONS

In the early part of this brief session, Andrea had spoken of her family. She touched on her dislike of the man living with them for the past twelve months. (Her parents are divorced.) This may well emerge again in later sessions. I sensed some intensity here, just under the brittle surface of her 'poised princess' charm. We also looked at the physiological link between hair loss and tension and the physiological effects of sitting on one's emotions.

Andrea seemed to understand this and to take it in for further reflection.

FIRST MAJOR SESSION

I begin by checking yesterday's perceptions, where Andrea appeared to be saying she was afraid she would lose all her hair and she feared teasing from her classmates.

B. 'Is that what we ought to work on today?'
A. 'It's not quite it.'
With much difficulty, she finally gets 'it' into words.
    'I've just got this worry that's always there. I can't get rid of it.'
B. 'Well, let's start with that. Choose something in the room to be this worry.'
Andrea looks startled, confused, self-conscious. She knows nothing of psychodrama. This is a strange idea to her. I make a playful, expansive gesture towards the dolls and puppets lolling around in armchairs, perched on heaters or hanging from bookshelves.
B. 'This is a wonderful room. Anything can happen here! I'm going to teach you a way of looking at a problem that's not just putting it into words. Have a good look around. Find something that can represent this worry of yours.'
Andrea looks intrigued and searches carefully, finally choosing a little hedgehog glove puppet with appealing face and spiky spines. She giggles.
B. 'Talk to this worry of yours.'
Andrea is intrigued, but silent.
B. 'Do you like it?'
A. 'No!'
B. 'Tell it.'
A. 'I don't like you.'
B. 'Why?'
A. 'Because you're always there.'
B. *[Doubling]* 'Yeah. You never leave me alone.'
A. 'You're there all the time. I can't get rid of you.'
She lapses into self-consciousness again.
B. 'Show with your body how it feels to have this worry with you all the time.'
Andrea is nonplussed. She has never been approached like this before.
B. 'It's a bit like miming.'

45

Andrea clearly does not know what mime is.
B demonstrates. Andrea remains very self-conscious. 'I can't open up to this', she seems to be saying.

B. 'Let's walk around with this worry that hangs on all the time.'
She takes her arm. They walk in a circle, with Andrea holding the 'worry' puppet.

B. 'What do you do about it when you're stuck with this blasted thing that won't go away?'

A. 'I keep with my friends, and I talk and listen to them talking, so that I can't think about my worries.'

B. 'So that's how you try to shake it off.'
She walks with her a little further.

'Show with your body how you try to shake off your worries.'
Andrea looks self-conscious. She does not respond. This kind of directive has no meaning for her.

B. 'Well, let's see if we can get this nameless worry clearer another way.'
She produces paper and suggests Andrea might draw it. Andrea looks very uncomfortable, and B continues to search for an adequate method to bring the elusive problem into the open.

B. 'You could use words instead of a drawing.'
Andrea appears more relaxed, but she is still 'stuck'.

B. 'Throw out on the paper the first word that comes into your mind when I say "worry".'
Andrea writes 'sad'.

B. 'So . . . it makes you sad. Throw out some more words.'
Andrea writes 'annoyed'.

B. *[Needing to check the facts]* 'You get irritable when you're worried?'
Andrea shakes her head. There are no words. Tears fill her eyes.
B abandons this point of clarification and responds to the intense feeling.

B. 'Something's bothering you right now. What's happening to you?'
Andrea stays helplessly dumb. B adds the words, 'locked up'. Shortly after this, Andrea writes 'happy'.

B. 'Why?'
Andrea's next response flows more freely. She writes 'Because I talked to you'.

B. 'Ah . . . so that was good . . . to talk about it. Have you ever talked to anyone else?'
Andrea shakes her head. She looks sad.

B. 'But you'd like to. . . . Why don't you?'

Andrea writes 'Can't find the words'.

B. 'Who would you like to talk to?'

Andrea sits there helplessly.

B. 'Throw out on the paper the names of the people you'd like to talk to.'

Andrea writes the names of four school friends.

B. 'Choose some toys to be these friends.'

Andrea moves with interest to choose appropriate figures. She settles on a rag doll with a cheeky face and long skinny arms and legs.

B. 'Who is that?'

A. 'Trudi.'

B. 'Where is she?'

A. 'On the oval.'

B. 'Put her there.'

Andrea carefully positions the doll so that she is sitting upright. Then, following similar directions, she chooses the others, taking delight in them and placing them carefully in a circle, just as girls do during lunch hour at school, talking endlessly of things both large and small.

B. 'Where are you? Choose a toy to be you?'

Andrea thinks for a while. She chooses a male punk doll with spiky purple hair and a safety pin in its ear. She holds the doll, standing apart from the group, looking sad and completely unable to express herself. Tears well up.

B. 'You're feeling sad?' *[A nods.]* 'Talk to your friends about the sadness.'

A. *[To friends]* 'You don't understand. Sometimes you make me angry.'

She stops short. Her face suggests she is thinking, but no words come. Her eyes fill with tears. She stands dejectedly.

B. 'This anger in you is all locked up. Show them how angry you are. Not with words; with your body.'

There is no response from her.

B. *[Doubling]* 'I'm feeling sad.' *[She shows it with her body language.]* 'And all alone. And I'm stuck. This worry that's always with me holds me back.'

She points to the puppet Andrea is holding.

B. 'Use the puppet. Show how it's holding you back.'

Andrea does not respond. She looks sad.

B. *[Doubling]* 'I'm all alone. I'm not going to try to reach you. I'm going to curl up in a ball where you can't reach me either.'

She curls up in a tight, unhappy ball in the chair opposite the porcelain doll with the scarf and the tear on its cheek.

B. 'I'll be like her.' *[She points to the doll.]*

After about a minute of mirroring Andrea's withdrawn, unhappy state, B stands and, as director again, says

'Come over here, to the chair, and be Andrea all locked up and alone.'

Andrea responds readily. She identifies with this role. She stays for some seconds, curled up in the chair.

B. 'What's coming up for you?'

Andrea's tears brim over.

B. 'You can't find the words?' *[A nods.]* 'Who is it you want to talk to?'

A. 'Trudi.'

B. 'Bring Trudi over.'

Andrea places the long-legged doll in sitting position on the floor in front of the chair.

B. 'I'll help you talk with Trudi. See . . . I'll BE Trudi.'

She sits where the doll was, and holds it in front of her.

B. 'Talk to me. Say what you want to say.'

A. 'Why won't you talk to me?'

B. 'Reverse roles with Trudi.'

They swap positions. Andrea does this with ease.

B. *[Repeats the question]* 'Why won't you talk to me?'

A. *[As Trudi, thinks long and hard, and looks unhappy.]*
'Because I can't help you.'

B. 'Reverse roles.'

B. *[Repeats Trudi's]* 'Because I can't help you.'

The words appear to affect Andrea deeply. She looks intently at Trudi, very tearful, and silent for quite a while. Then she says

A. 'You think if you leave me alone, I'll stop being un-happy.'

In an aside to B, as director, she says

'In our group, whenever one of us is unhappy the others talk about it and help the one who's unhappy. But they don't talk to me about my hair.'

B. 'Reverse roles.'

'You think if you leave me alone, I'll stop being unhappy.'

Andrea listens, as Trudi, to the words. She replies

'Yes . . . sometimes I do.'

B. 'Reverse roles.'

Andrea is quite overwhelmed when B, as Trudi, repeats this to her. She weeps. There are no words.

B. *[As director, moves over to where Andrea is huddled in the chair.]* 'You feel very alone when Trudi says this?'

Andrea nods. She tries to speak. Her fingers flutter to her lips. She mouths a word. . . . No sound comes. . . . She repeats this several times.

B. *[Squatting close to her, her voice at once comforting and challenging]* 'You want to say something, but the words are all locked up?'

Andrea nods, tearfully.

B. *[Commandingly]* 'Say what you want to say to Trudi!'

Again, Andrea mouths the beginning of a word, fingers fluttering again, the process repeated again.

B. 'The words are there. I see them coming.'

She gestures with her hand near the tip of her tongue, mirroring Andrea's inarticulate desire to express herself.

B. *[Commandingly]* 'Let them out!'

A. 'Trudi! Please talk to me!'

Her voice is strong, authoritative. A look of immense relief comes over her face.

B. 'There! You've found the words you wanted!'

She gives Andrea a little hug.

'Shall we stop there for today?' *[A nods.]* 'It feels a good place to stop?'

Andrea smiles and nods. Her face looks like a garden where there's sun after rain. There's no need for more words.

B. 'Let's put the toys back. We don't need them any more to be Andrea, and Trudi, and . . .'

She names each one as Andrea picks it up, allowing her to de-role the toys and to defuse the power they took on during the session. As they leave the room, B says

'You know, I think there's another thing that's stopping Trudi from talking to you about all this. She probably does think she can't help you. But also, maybe she doesn't know how much you need to let those tears out. She doesn't have to stop the tears, but she probably doesn't know that yet. Maybe she just doesn't know what to do. . . . You might have to help her.'

Andrea nods thoughtfully. Her face is peaceful and smiling as she leaves.

The next session with Andrea was brief (about twenty minutes) as she was heading off for some cross-country running with her school-mates. It followed a more traditional counselling format, with some use of the 'words on paper' technique that had helped to unlock her a little in the previous session. We centred on her reactions to her parents' separation about four years earlier. She was clearly fond of her father, seeing him at irregular intervals because of his job as an interstate sales representative. But he kept in touch with her constantly and was an important person to her. She wished her parents would live together again so that they would be an ordinary family. ('All the kids I go round with have both their parents.') We discussed the dream of a restored family.

She strongly resented Bob's presence in the family. He was a high-flying company director, who came to live with them a year ago. The 'words on paper' technique revealed that Andrea believed Bob was one of the friends who had talked her mother into separating from her husband. The children (Andrea and her two younger sisters) disliked him because he made new rules in the home (and, I suspect, because they saw him as a usurper). She never talked with her mother about this. I suggested she could have a time here in this room where I could help her talk with her mother about what it's like when your parents are separated.

TWO-HOUR SESSION WITH ANDREA AND HER MOTHER

I originally intended to give about one hour to this, but new, emotionally charged material suddenly emerged as we were finishing off and I decided to follow it.

I begin the session by asking Mrs X and Andrea each separately to create a sculpture, using any objects in the room, to depict the way they communicate with each other. Although this is new to them, they latch on to the idea without much more explanation. Mrs X's sculpture shows an adult female doll with a bowl and a small child doll sitting near-by. It represents a time when Andrea likes to talk to her – learning how to cook. Andrea arranges the punk doll, a small girl doll and a cat watching an adult doll working. Her sculpture represents herself and her sister, with their cat, watching Mrs X gardening. Both sculptures represent a time of emotional closeness.

B. 'It's interesting . . . both of you have chosen a time when you're either communicating without words or talking about something that's not very personal. And yet you both have very personal things on your minds.'

It emerges that they both find the presence of Andrea's younger sister an obstacle to personal conversations. We look at their passivity regarding this – no attempts have been made to set up good one-to-one scenes for themselves.

B. 'I don't think that's the main reason why you don't talk'. *[To Mrs X]* 'Andrea is one of the world's greatest bottlers of feelings and I wouldn't mind betting you're the same. One subject that I suspect you've both bottled is the changes in the family over the past few years. . . . Andrea, you were talking to me about some of your problems the other day. Do you think you could talk to Mum about them?'

With great difficulty, Andrea begins to speak of Bob.

A. 'He's so bossy. He doesn't take any notice of how we used to live before he came. He just tells us what to do. Like the washing-up. He says who has to do it. We used to take it in turns.'

It is hard for Andrea to say all this to her mother. Her voice is hesitant. Her eyes keep filling with tears. Mrs X sits at a distance, her face perfectly composed, body straight, not a hair out of place. Andrea might as well be a television newsreader predicting another sunny autumn day tomorrow.

Mrs X. 'Well, you have to understand it's hard for Bob. He has a busy job and he's very tired when he comes home. He just wants things to run smoothly. He doesn't know that you used to . . .

B. *[Cuts across Mrs X's composed explaining away of Bob's behaviour and A's outwardly submissive acceptance of this. She doubles, bobbing down behind A and speaking for her.]* 'Yuk!!! Fat lot of good that does for me! You're just sticking up for HIM! What about me? Can't you see I'm crying? Yuk!!!'

Andrea laughs, identifying with this rebellion and anger. They both remain stiffly separate in their far-apart chairs, however, and the discussion remains stilted.

B. 'I don't know about you, but I want a cup of coffee. I'll go and get some while you talk this through. Who wants a cup?' *[Mrs X does, A doesn't.]*

B returns to the room, knocking on the door with her foot, her hands occupied in holding the cups. There's a small pause. Mrs X opens the door, then resumes her seat far away from the still wet-eyed Andrea.

B. *[Challenges them for their denial of emotion]* To Mrs X. 'You're sitting there, looking very composed. Andrea is still obviously upset and there are yards of space between you. Most mothers, who love their kids as much as I know you love Andrea, couldn't cope with staying so separate. I thought, when I went out of the room, that you both might have done something about it.'

Mrs X. 'We did. Andrea ended up in my lap.'

B. 'But you scurried back there before I came in?'

They laugh – caught out. B laughs too.

B. 'Well, let's bring the chairs together. Make a sort of couch.'

Mrs X. 'It might be easier if we sit on the floor.'

She and Andrea end up there, arms around each other. B sits close to them, a little to the side, also on the floor. She spends a little time assisting them to look at, and label, their submissiveness to authority figures (or people they perceive as such) and their withholding of pain-inflicting emotion.

B. 'It seems to me that one thing you need to talk about is what you each believe to be the reason for the family's splitting up.' *[To Mrs X]* 'Have you ever told Andrea?' *[She shakes her head.]* 'I think she'd find it helpful to know.'

Mrs X then tells a long story of unhappiness and of being left time and time again to cope with the family on her own while her husband went off, with no discussion, to give himself extended holidays. As she speaks of her loneliness and her feeling of being de-valued, she weeps, and Andrea comforts her with hugs and stroking.

B. 'So . . . that's not quite the way you thought it was, was it? Tell Mum what you thought had happened.'

Andrea then outlines her image of her mother making new friends while her father was away working, with one of these friends becoming someone she liked better. She is surprised to learn her mother had not met Bob until a year later. Mrs X, in turn, is surprised to learn Andrea had this misconception. Their relating is immediate and uninhibited. They both show, in their body language and especially in their radiantly freed-up faces, that this new closeness is good.

B. 'You're lucky to have been able to talk with your Mum like this and to have her tell you her thoughts and show you her sadness. Lots of girls can't talk to their mothers. Lots of grown-up women can't either. I wanted to talk to my Mum once about something that really mattered to me, but she couldn't handle it. She walked away. And my Dad wasn't there. He'd died . . .'

At this, Mrs X breaks into deep sobbing.

B. 'Something very deep is coming up for you?'

Mrs X nods.

Mrs X. *[Sobbing]* 'It's my parents.' *[She is unable to go on.]*

B knows that Mrs X's mother has multiple sclerosis and her father has a serious heart condition. They both need a great deal of care.

B. 'They're not there . . . for you?'

Mrs X then goes on to express her deep feeling of aloneness. Her parents are alive, but they are not there for her. Her mother is absorbed by her own illness. Her father may not have long to live. Neither of them must be upset. So she protects and supports them, and hides her fears and needs from them as well as from her children (and, I suspect, from Bob).

Andrea's handling of all this is very moving. She is staggered to find her mother expressing so much emotion, and she comforts her wordlessly throughout – her arm around her, her hand caressing her. We look at family patterns of holding back feeling, of not asking for needed comfort, and (for Mrs X) of carrying the world on her shoulders and hiding her own painful needs under a smooth-browed front of serenity. We look at the parallels with Andrea and the strong possibility that her hair-loss problem would be helped if she learned to break this pattern. I lean forward a little to touch their knees, allowing them to see that my own eyes are not entirely dry.

B. 'I feel very moved being part of this . . . Andrea . . . I look at you, with your arms so comfortingly around your Mum, with your face sort of shining with love for her. You're not using words, are you? They're good sometimes, but you can communicate very well without them if you use the rest of yourself – the way you're doing now. Not being able to find the words isn't **always** a problem.'

Andrea needed little further work with me. Her hair gradually grew back. I learned later that she coped very well with the transition to High School. Some years later, she and her mother read this account of their session with great interest. The fear and loneliness of those days seemed far away, and life was good.

There may well have been other factors influencing the retreat of Andrea's alopecia problem, and this account of her therapy with me is not part of a carefully controlled research project.

Bearing that in mind, however, it is still interesting to note that similar re-growth occurred for another younger child with alopecia. She, too, had accessed what seemed to be at the centre of some inner confusion and turmoil, again related to her parents' separation. (According to her mother, the incident the child was exploring had occurred just before the first signs of hair loss.) Rossi (1980) makes some interesting comments in relation to psychosomatic illness and the value of short-term therapy that focusses on the client's immediate life-situation rather than on the distant past. He claims

> The establishment of a new and propitious balance of personality forces sometimes even very slight, may tip the scales in favor of a spontaneous, progressive recovery similar to the natural biological healing that frequently results from the removal of a single element in an organic disease complex. All of this is in accord with the experience of everyday life, wherein a single, seemingly insignificant, stimulus or experience can shatter or establish the destiny of an individual or even a nation.

> (Rossi 1980:xix)

For these two girls, the scales were certainly tipped in favour of spontaneous recovery. Whatever else in their lives contributed to their cure is open to speculation, however, and we need to remember these are only two cases – not enough to provide material for general conclusions.

Meanwhile, Andrea's own story stands as an example of courageous willingness to follow unfamiliar paths in search of healing.

6

MICHAEL

Michael was a much younger child with special needs who required a different approach. Through teaching me that therapeutic stories have a power that can backfire, he set me on a new road. I began to develop a style that linked storytelling with the psychodramatic principles I had been able to use more directly with Andrea.

Michael was a seven-year-old with a severe language disorder that had prevented him from learning the simple grammatical constructs necessary for normal speech. Because his expressive language was so limited, it was often difficult to know how much he had absorbed in a conversation. The speech pathologist working with him believed Michael had reached a plateau in his work with her, partly because he needed to work through his feelings about his mother's death eighteen months earlier. He had said goodbye to her as usual in the morning when he left for school. In the afternoon she wasn't there. A car accident had resulted in instant death. At that time, Michael was not receiving treatment for his language disorder and his relatives did not know he could understand spoken language. So little was done to help him understand what had happened. His confusion and grief remained locked up in the largely silent world he knew.

The speech pathologist knew of some simple storytelling I'd been doing for some time, using puppets and basing the stories on the everyday hassles that children have. She asked me to work with Michael on the issue of grieving. He had never talked about his mother and resisted anyone who tried to coax him.

In creating a story for him, I needed to feel my way into his world and imagine the impact of such a shattering of his hitherto predictable little life. I wanted the story to deal with the grieving process, and to contain key elements of his own experiences, but it needed to be sufficiently distanced to allow him to enjoy it as simple entertainment if he was not ready to allow his grieving process to surface. So it needed to be able to stand as a story in its own right.

THE STORYTELLING SESSION

Michael chooses six friends to come across the school's playing field to the room where I then worked. I allow them to run around for a while, discovering all the puppets and dolls and playing freely for a few minutes.

B. 'Okay, time for our story. Put the puppets quietly in your laps and we'll see which of them we need . . .'
She chooses the adult female doll with the tear on its cheek. She sits on the storyteller's chair, the doll on her knee, its tear-stained cheek hidden against her shoulder. She looks at the doll intently.
B. 'Why, you're crying!'
Woman Doll   *[With B speaking for her and manipulating her movements and gestures.]* 'No, I'm not!!'
B. 'You **are**.' *[Her voice is full of sympathy.]* 'What's the matter?'
Woman Doll   'Nothing's the matter! I'm **not** crying!'
She digs her tear-stained cheek further into the storyteller's shoulders. B picks up a little girl doll, with long, spindly, double-jointed arms and legs and appealingly cheeky face. She brings the little girl doll forward and invites one of the children to make the doll use its hands to turn the woman's head around. The tear clearly shows.
Little Girl Doll   *[With B speaking for her]* 'It's all right to cry. . . . You're allowed to cry. . . . People cry when they're sad . . . and when they're sad, it's good for them to talk about it.' *[She gently wipes the tear.]* 'What's the matter? . . . Tell me.'
Woman Doll   'My little cat has gone. He ran down to the gate with me when I went to work yesterday morning, the way he always does. But when I came home, he was gone, and I haven't seen him since . . . and maybe I'll never see him again.'
She weeps freely.
Little Girl Doll   'Oh, how sad!' *[She puts her arm around her.]* 'When you've lost someone you love, it sometimes makes you feel a bit better if you talk about it. . . . Tell me about your cat? What's his name?'

Woman Doll 'Midnight.'

Little Girl Doll 'And what does he look like?'

Woman Doll 'He's beautiful. His coat is shiny and black. His eyes are huge and green. He's got the longest whiskers in the world.'

B picks up the echidna glove puppet.

Echidna 'I know Midnight. He used to chase me. But he was scared of my prickles.'

B picks up the punk doll.

Punk 'Midnight used to rub around my legs. I liked him.' *[Gruffly]* 'I'm sorry you're sad.' *[He pats her head shyly.]*

B. *[To the children holding the other toys]* 'Do any of you know Midnight?'

Children 'Yes.'

B. 'What do you want to say? What do you want to do?'

She encourages the children to add to the story. They join in with zest, ad libbing freely . . .

B. *[When the children have run out of ideas, she speaks for the possum.]* 'Sometimes I'm scared of Midnight . . . but I wish he could be here. I don't want you to be sad. I'll help you look for him.'

B. 'Let's all look for him.'

Holding their puppets, the children hunt around the room and finally find the black cat, joyfully restoring it to its owner. Everyone joins in the happy reuniting of Midnight and the woman.

I told the speech pathologist I was not at all sure that this little story would have special implications for Michael or that he was capable of generalizing it to his own situation. But from then on, the integration aide working with him in his classroom noted that his drawings all began to contain a line across the middle, with people above it and others below. 'What's the line for?' she asked. Michael pointed to the people above it. 'Those people dead. . . . That's Mum. . . . That's Grandpa. . . . That's Mr X.' Every day, for some weeks he brought his mother into his pictures and talked about her.

Then came a development that highlighted an important omission in my work with Michael. Unaware, at that stage, of just how powerfully children can use therapeutic stories, I had not thought to tell his father the purpose of my storytelling. Michael came to school one day, unusually quiet and unusually obedient. The integration aide asked if he was ill. After some days of this out-of-character behaviour from Michael, the aide checked with his family. She learned that his favourite uncle had died suddenly from a heart attack. When Michael was told, he said: 'Want to see him'. When told this was not possible, he repeated 'Want to see him! Want to say goodbye! Uncle Jim heaven. Mummy heaven. No say goodbye Mummy. Say goodbye Uncle Jim!' There was no-one in his family who understood the depth of his need and no-one knew how to comfort him. It was left to the integration aide to put her arms around him and let him talk.

I never again underestimated the power of therapeutic stories. Since then, I always worked closely with parents in the planning of the story, the telling of it (often inviting them to be present), and in following up any behavioural changes that occurred. And the story itself had a closer link with psychodramatic principles.

Round about that time, I observed that psychodrama and children's play both have much in common with the structure of the classic fairy tale. In the fairy tale, there are heroes and villains, a difficult task or life-goal, great adventures and struggles and finally victory and a joyful celebration. In psychodrama, there are several parallels: enactments that depict the protagonist's strengths and weaknesses; elements of his inner world and social environment that help or hinder his carrying out of a desired role; the release of spontaneity leading to catharsis and the discovery of new solutions.

The stories that evolved from these observations were built around what I had come to believe (usually through several sessions of therapy) to be the absolute centre of the child's problem. The protagonist in the story was a fictional creature whose adventures paralleled a difficulty faced by the child. As in fairy tales, there were characters who assisted and others who obstructed the protagonist's pursuit of a life-enhancing goal. They represented the strengths and weaknesses in the child's existing coping mechanisms. Often the child would interrupt the story and create a happy ending. His face, at key points in the story, was my guide, telling me when my hypothesis regarding his problem was in line with his view of reality.

My work with Michael was limited to this single storytelling session. I moved into private practice soon afterwards and lost contact with the referring speech pathologist. So, for me,

Michael's own story is an unfinished one. All I know is that he absorbed a great deal from that playful session with his friends and he wove it into the texture of his life.

7

MEG

Six-year-old Meg was a born storyteller herself, and the way in which her story was created was somewhat different. Unlike Michael, she had no problems with language and she was very free in her play. So it was possible to draw her in as co-narrator from time to time. She had been referred by her mother, who was worried to find her outgoing little daughter's moods swinging between depression and uncharacteristic bursts of anger and defiance. Meg's mother, Sally, noticed this happened after access visits to her father. The therapeutic story that sprang into our second session was, in one sense, not planned. There was no time to check it with her mother, since it came into being as we worked, and was a direct response to some withdrawn behaviour from Meg. But, in another sense, it *was* planned. I had already given her situation a good deal of thought, attempting to imagine my way into it.

With each child I see, the work begins with an interview with the parents or care-givers. From the wealth of information that emerges (the situation that has given rise to the referral; the parents' view of the child's characteristics and strengths; social groups and people who have an influence on the child's life, etc.) I try to imagine what is at the heart of the problem for the child. From *her* perspective, regardless of the view others may take, what is at the very centre? Meg was already expressing, clearly and vehemently, her unwillingness to visit her father. Her parents had separated shortly after her birth and she had never bonded with her father. He himself was ambivalent about her visits and did not find his time with her easy to handle. Meg was caught in the legal web of her parents' divorce terms. It was a powerless position. And she was a little girl who liked to be in charge of her own affairs as much as possible.

With this in mind, I had formed some tentative hypotheses about the central issues for Meg before I met her. But they were only hypotheses, and I was prepared to abandon them if she herself came up with other concerns.

FIRST SESSION

I welcome them at the door. Meg and her mother enter the room. Meg sits near her mother, but separate. She puts her thumb in her mouth, sticks her legs out in front of her on the floor, looks up at me cautiously. I check with Sally. What has she told Meg about the purpose of her visit to my house? We establish that Meg knows her mother met me one day. Sally learned that I have lots of toys and that children who've been a bit unhappy about something often come to play. That's the best way for children to feel okay again. Sally knew Meg was often angry and unhappy lately, so she brought her here to play.

I invite Meg to look at the toys at the side of the room. She's interested, but her body still expresses caution. I then tell her there are more in the cupboard. I open the door. Meg gasps with joy 'Oh!' and immediately starts exploring them in freedom.

At this point I suggest to her mother that she might leave Meg and me to play if she has other things she needs to do. She says she wants to go to the shops. We arrange that she'll return in about forty-five minutes. Meg is quite relaxed about this, quietly exploring the toys while we talk. We're left together.

B. 'Okay. Let's have some games. You can be the boss of the first game' [this in response to her very purposeful, assertive body language] 'and I'll be the boss of the second.'
Meg seizes a king figure.
M. 'We'll have the Mary story.'
B. 'Oh . . . all right. . . . You tell me what to do . . . it's your game.'
M. 'This can be Mary. . . . ' [Looks around fruitlessly.] 'Have you got something for Joseph?'
B. [Also looking – there are no adequate males around. She offers the punk doll doubtfully.] 'Would this do?'
M. [Shocked] 'No!! He's got ear-rings.'
She looks round for a while and settles for a furry rat or possum puppet.
'This is Joseph.'

B accepts this totally seriously and the game goes on. . . . Finally B says
'Can we finish this off now, so that I can be the boss of the next game?'

Meg accepts this quite readily. Mary and Joseph and the baby (a stone wrapped in rag) gallop off on the donkey.

B. 'Let's play a game where you show me the people in your family. . . . Choose something to be you.'

Meg chooses the best: the doll with the porcelain head. We arrange her centre stage.

B. 'Choose something to be Mum.'

Meg chooses the only toy that's larger than the white-faced doll – the panther.

B. 'Choose something to be Dad.'

M. *[Alarmed]* 'I can't! He doesn't live with us.'

B. 'That's okay. . . . He lives in a different house. . . . Let's make a house for you and Mum.'

Meg does this with some chairs. She puts them in.

B. 'Let's make a different house for Dad.'

M. 'He lives with Grandma.'

B. 'Choose something to be Grandma.'

M. *[Chooses swiftly – a pretty 'good-girl' doll.]* 'Grandma's a sweet little thing' *she confides to me over her shoulder. (M's mother has already told me she's painfully good.)*

B. 'Choose something to be Dad.'

M. *[Going towards the cupboard dragging her feet a little.]* 'He's a horrible man.' *[Her face wrinkles with distaste as she tries to choose. She finally pulls out a clown.]* 'You'll do! I don't like your shirt.' *[She throws the clown on the floor.]*

B. 'Let's make it you're going to visit your Dad.'

M. 'I don't like going to his place. He puts mud on my face. And he throws me in the pool.'

B. 'That doesn't sound very nice. Do you tell him you don't like it?'

M. 'No.'

B. 'Why not?'

M. 'Because my body tells me not to.'

B. *[Understanding totally]* 'Oh.'

M. *[Suddenly jumps up.]* 'This story has to have a happy ending!'

B. *[Joins in her enthusiasm.]* 'Hurray! Let's have a happy ending!'

M. *[She takes the clown by the leg and throws him down fiercely.]* 'You're dead!'

This totally unexpected 'happy ending' leaves B with a dilemma. Such a move by a protagonist in an adult psychodrama would be maximized by the director and would probably become a highlight of the drama. The adult would remain clear in perceiving that the director, in doing this, is not wishing the actual death of the person. Would Meg become confused if B built up the scene in the usual way? If B failed to respond to her feelings, would she feel rebuked for having expressed a 'death wish' in the game? B decides to express mock horror and shock, clowning her response with exaggerated mime. In this way, the 'play' quality of the enactment is emphasized, at the same time as the horror of the thought is acknowledged and permission is given to act it out in the game. Meg is encouraged. The suppressed anger is allowed to surface further in play.

M. 'And what's more, you're going to hell! *[She stands over him as she shouts this.]*

B. *[Increases her shock-horror reaction]* 'It sounds as if we ought to choose a spot for hell so that you can put him there.'

Meg chooses the cupboard where the toys are kept. B encourages her to shut the door.

B. 'Let's celebrate the happy ending. How shall we celebrate?'

M. *[Firmly]* 'We'll dance.'

She puts on dress-up clothes and does a ballerina's dance, slowly, seriously, aware she's centre-stage.

SECOND VISIT

I ask Meg what she'd like to play today. She sits there, dejected, passive – and shrugs.

B. 'When your Mum brought you here last week, she said you were sometimes unhappy. But you're not always unhappy. How about you draw me a picture about Meg when she's happy? Would you like to do that?'

Meg agrees and I set her up at a little table with paper and texta colours. She draws a buoyant picture of herself surrounded by flowers, birds and a rainbow.

M. 'I'll do some writing.' *[With great concentration she writes]* 'I me Meg' 'How do you spell 'because'?'

B. 'B-E-C-A-U-S-E'

Meg writes 'because I me born'. B spends time enjoying her picture and her writing with her.

While she was drawing, I was considering ways of helping her retrieve the release she had at the end of her play last week. I'm now interpreting the dejected behaviour as coming from a sense of guilt that she has broken a taboo in her death-wish for her father. I try to find a therapeutic story that is sufficiently distanced to be unthreatening and that gives her permission to be very angry when she's treated badly by adults who expect her to respect them.

I also weave in an analogy to her powerless situation whereby (because her parents have reached a legal agreement regarding access) she has to endure contact with a person she dislikes.

MEG'S STORY

Once upon a time there was a little old woman who lived in a beautiful forest with her grand-daughter.

I get Meg to choose dolls to represent Granny and the little girl and I ask her to make up a name for the little girl . . . Lisa.

One day, when the old woman was walking in the forest, a storm blew up. The wind howled, the rain poured, and the trees lashed around wildly, bending now this way, now that, until they thought they'd break. Suddenly there was a loud 'Crack'! Down came a branch, right on top of Lisa's Granny. Luckily she wasn't hurt, but she was pinned to the ground, unable to move, for the branch was large and very, very heavy.

'Oh, whatever will I do? What will become of me?' cried the old woman. 'Help! Help me, someone. Help!!'

Just then, she felt the earth shaking under her – thump, thump, thump. The Giant was hurrying home to get out of the rain.

'Oh, Mr Giant, please help me!' said Granny. 'You're big and strong. You could easily lift this branch off me. Please help me!'

But the Giant only laughed. He thought it was funny to see her trapped under the tree.

'Please, Mr Giant! My little grand-daughter is at home all by herself. She needs me. Please help me to get up!'

'Hmm', thought the Giant. 'Little grand-daughter?' You see, sometimes the Giant looked down from his castle and noticed the people with children having happy times. And he sometimes wished he had a child. Not for always. Oh, no!

Children were hard to put up with for always. But just sometimes. Maybe once a week? No. Once a month would be better.

'Well', said the Giant, 'I'll help you if you promise me one thing.'

'Anything, Anything. I'll promise you anything', said the little old woman. (By now her back was aching as if it would break in two, and her head was aching with worry about Lisa.)

'I'll lift the branch if you promise to let your grand-daughter come and stay with me for a whole day once a month.'

The old woman agreed. . . . And so it happened that Lisa had to visit the Giant every month.

Here I got Meg involved in the story. We set up the Giant's Castle – my swivel chair – and we have Lisa coming unwillingly up the path. Meg is then invited to make up what happened next. She has the Giant put mud on Lisa's face and throw her in the swimming pool. I pick up the story then, having Lisa return home feeling very unhappy.

That night she wouldn't eat her dinner. She threw the vegetables across the room and yelled at her Granny till she had to be sent to her room. The next day she was just as bad. *Here Meg helps me think of more terrible things Lisa did.*

Finally Granny could bear no more. 'Go outside and stay outside until you know how to behave', she shouted. 'I don't know what's come over you. You're not the girl you used to be!'

Lisa ran out into the garden and sat under a bush feeling sad and angry all at once. She was still there when Owl flew by.

'What's the matter with you?' asked Owl. 'You're looking very down in the dumps.'

Lisa told him how naughty she'd been and how muddled up her feelings were.

'Hmm', said Owl. 'I saw you up at the Giant's place yes-terday. You didn't look as though that was much fun. I think you're really very angry about that still and you're letting out your feelings at home.'

'Well, it's no use letting them out with the Giant', said Lisa. 'He'd get angry then and I'd be very frightened.'

'What you need is a friend', said Owl.

I get Meg to choose a friend. She chooses Banana Jim, the monkey.

'Next time you have to go to the Giant's place, I'll send Jimmy along too', said Owl.

Again I involve Meg in creating the story. Banana Jim ends up with a crowd of helpers who all encourage Lisa to tell the Giant she didn't like it when he put mud on her face and threw her in the pool.

All Lisa's other friends ended up doing the same to the Giant, putting mud on his face and throwing him into the pool. The Giant roared and cried and got very upset as he splashed around in the pool. This time, when Lisa returned home, Owl taught her not to sit under a bush moping when she remembered the bad bits about her visit to the Giant's home.

'While you're doing that, the whole beautiful world is passing you by, and you don't even notice', said Owl. 'Come here.'

And he put her under a beautiful flowering tree.

I get Meg to sit under a flowered parasol.

'Look at all the creatures who are enjoying this beautiful world.'

We then have a parade of the sort of animals, birds and plants that had been in Meg's drawing.

And the sun beamed on her and bent to make a rainbow, and Lisa stopped moping and became her happy self again, laughing at the little rabbit's antics and reaching out her hands with joy at the rainbow. Owl flew down and kissed her cheek, and said,

'There! You're learning to be as wise as I am!'

There were several moments in the telling of this story when Meg's eyes widened and she became very still. Her body language expressed recognition that this story was for her. One such time was when Owl taught her to sit under the beautiful flowering tree rather than stay moping under the bush. When Owl flew down and kissed her cheek with his soft felt beak, she blushed with pleasure and looked up at me as she accepted his compliment. She visited me twice more. There was no need to spell out any of the implications of the story. She made her own connections and her parents noticed changes in her behaviour. She let her father know her wishes when he was unrealistic in his demands on her and she managed this in a way that was acceptable to him. The exaggerated acting out in a therapeutic play setting had released her ability to come up with workable solutions in real life. And at home her temper outbursts and fits of depression died away.

8

JESSICA

Jessica remained a shadowy figure for me. In deference to her extreme fear of revealing herself, I shall leave her own story untold, except to say that it had been full of changes and moves that were all outside her control. I was one of a long line of professionals she had encountered. She played with me with great caution, and her need to control every aspect of our time together remained immutable. There were circumstances in her life that made it difficult for me to offer anything of great value to her, so I gave her this story.

THE LITTLE ECHIDNA

Once upon a time, there was a great flood, and the rivers swelled and poured out over their banks and rushed in a great hurry on their path to the sea. And many of the forest animals were swept along with them.

Jessica helps me choose the animals, and I allow the Cockatoo and the Possum and the Frog to swirl out of sight.

Nobody knew what happened to them. Perhaps they did not survive. But one little Echidna was determined to live. He clung tenaciously to an overhanging branch of a tree and finally managed to clamber up on it. He lay there, exhausted, for a very long time, and then made his way to dry land. He remembered what his mother had taught him.

'When you're in danger, curl up into a tight little ball, and put your prickles up.'

Well, he certainly was in danger now. So he curled up tight, protecting the soft part of himself from further harm.

(You see, he'd already been hurt quite often as he hurtled down the river, banging against rocks, feeling the sharp edges of fallen trees, and his underbelly was torn and bleeding.)

Finally, the sun came out again, and other animals began moving around.

Jessica helps me choose them.

A Dingo came up and sniffed at the strange little ball. The hard prickles stuck in his nose and he gave a howl of pain as he streaked up the hill. A short time later, a wandering Cow came over to investigate. Once again, the little Echidna protected himself with his prickles, and the Cow went lumbering off, bellowing with surprise.

As time went on, the forest animals gradually realized that the hard little ball was real – it was an animal, just like themselves. They wanted to play with the Echidna, and they tried to coax him to uncurl. But he was still afraid. How did he know whether they were enemies or friends? Better to stay as he was, curled up small and safe. The animals asked Owl to help.

'What can we do to make him uncurl, Owl? It can't be good for him to stay like that forever.'

Owl moved her glasses up and down a few times and tried to look important and full of knowledge.

'Poke him', she said. 'Do it gently. But poke him. All of you.' So they did, taking it in turns. But the little Echidna stayed curled up, in a tight, hard little ball.

'Well', said Owl. 'Maybe my cousin, Magical Owl, will know what to do. Let's ask him.'

So they all trouped along to the mountain where Magical Owl lived.

I drape some beautifully coloured silken cloths over a heap of cushions in the swivel chair, and sit Magical Owl on top. He is full of extraordinary colours himself, nothing like the owls that usually live in the forest. Jessica helps me arrange the animals as they climb up the mountain-side.

Possum spoke up and told Magical Owl how worried they were about this little animal that stayed curled up.

'We'd like to play with him', said Possum. 'But he puts his prickles into us if we go too near.'

Magical Owl listened, and nodded, and finally spoke.

69

'Come closer to me, where you can hear, and I'll tell you what you must do', he said.

The animals crowded round and waited expectantly. At last, Magical Owl spoke.

'Wait', he said. And that was all. . . . The animals looked at each other doubtfully. Had they heard aright? Wait?

'Yes', said Magical Owl. 'Wait . . . until he's not afraid any more. And then he will uncurl.'

And Magical Owl drooped his head into his soft, downy breast and seemed to go to sleep. The animals filed silently down the mountain, full of amazement. Magical Owl called to the sun and asked her to shine on the little Echidna . . . And she did. Her warm rays reached him, past all the prickles, past all the hurt, deep into his heart.

I invite Jessica to stand there as the sun and to hold her arms out in warmth over him.

And slowly, slowly, the little Echidna began to feel better. Slowly, slowly, he began to uncurl. He turned over on his back . . . cautiously . . . and let the sun's warm rays reach the soft part of his body.

Here Jessica abandons the standing pose I had taught her. She moves gently over to the Echidna, squatting beside him and letting her hands move tenderly just above the surface of his body.

And after a very long time, the forest animals came close. With great care, they licked the Echidna's wounds and then left him lying peacefully in the sun, waiting for the time when he would be ready to play.

There were some reasons why I needed to discontinue working with Jessica, for a while, at least. But I told her she could come back any time she wanted. It may be she will choose not to do this. However, she has taken my story with her. We had two more sessions before she left, and she asked if she could be the echidna in a story she wanted to make. She spent a long time experiencing the tightness of the spiky little glove puppet as she held him curled around her closed fist, and in her story he went on to enjoy games with his new playmates. I'm not sure if she understood all that I was telling her of my belief in the importance of survival strategies, and the necessity of letting go of them when it is time, but I strongly suspect she did.

9

MARK

Mark was an eight-year-old boy who had been referred to me by a colleague. Some six months earlier, Mark's father had lost his temper and had beaten him uncontrollably, to the point where the child needed hospital attention and the father was placed on probation. Prior to the session recorded here, I had obtained as much background information as possible, to give me an understanding of Mark's whole social setting, and I'd spent time with his father, attempting to absorb the extent of his very real remorse regarding the incident. We agreed on the way he should tell Mark why he wanted him to meet me. I then spent time reflecting on all I had learned, making some tentative hypotheses as to what kind of inner world this child might be in the process of constructing, and what expectations or apprehensions might be filling his mind as he came to our meeting. Before opening the door to them, I put myself in touch with the child within me. I was ready for our first time together. I expected we would play, and I would give Mark as much freedom to play as he willed. In this way, we would both spend some undemanding time getting to know each other and I would obtain valuable clues as to the landscape of his inner world. All this followed the usual pattern of my work with a new child. And all went as imagined until Mark found the panther. Immediately, he and I were in unmapped territory.

Let us go back in time a little, to the point where they entered the room, with Mark's whole bearing expressing openness and eagerness. I ask his father what he has told Mark about the purpose of his visit. He shrugs helplessly. He had lost his nerve (or the words), it seems. With some assistance, he finally finds the way to express himself. 'Well, since that time I lost my temper badly with you, we haven't been such good mates. I want to get

71

back to us being good mates.' Mark listens wide-eyed, open, trusting. He nods. I move on to talk about the toys in the room and how I use them with children. He explores some of the puppets with me. Then I open the cupboard to reveal rows and rows of them, sitting, lying, hanging, swinging. 'Wow!' he says. And the moment is right for me to suggest his father leave us for a while to play.

As he leaves, Mark is already exploring the next cupboard. He pulls out a large brown panther, and immediately begins a frenzy of bashing, knocking him to the ground and kicking him savagely time and time again. All this is done with wild energy and enjoyment. Meanwhile, as director, I am taken aback. No child before has by-passed the preliminaries so swiftly. I experience a sense of shock at the intensity of his aggression and his obvious readiness to enter a therapeutic experience. For some time I allow him the catharsis of acting out the aggressor's role, then decide to deepen the experience by attempting to involve him in a form of role reversal.

B. [*Doubling for Panther, lying beside him and groaning, crying, sobbing, pleading. Then, as director and in standing position, saying to Mark*] 'He needs help! Find someone who can help him!'
Mark, not to be distracted, continues the bashing. B chooses other toys as rescuers and attempts to intervene. Mark bashes them all, becoming more and more excited. B makes a therapeutic decision to contain this energy and assist Mark to move it in another direction. As director, she stands at full height, with full authority in eyes, body and voice.
B. 'Then I will protect him!'
Mark moves to hit her.
B. 'Oh, no! No-one hits me.'
Mark moves again.
B. 'No!! In this room, I am the one who will stop this person from damaging Panther. I will not allow anyone to lose control to that degree, and to damage somebody so badly.'
Mark's eyes reflect a change. He is now identifying with the Panther.
B. [*With full authority*] 'You must help! QUICKLY! What will we do for Panther?'
M. 'We'll put him to bed.'
B. 'Good. Get the bed.'
Mark arranges the door-rug.
B. 'Wonderful . . . just what he needs . . . put him to bed.'

Mark gathers up the Panther with exquisite tenderness and carries him to the rug, laying him down gently.

B. *[Doubling for Panther]*: 'Oh . . . Oh . . . Thank you . . . Oh . . . That's better . . . Oh . . . Oh . . .

B. *[As Director]* 'Who can help him? Get someone to help him.'

Mark goes to the cupboard, returning with a large white seal.

B. 'Oh, hello! Who are you?'

M. 'I'm the doctor.'

B. 'Thank goodness you're here, Dr Seal. He needs a doctor. Come this way.'

Mark arranges the Seal, makes him stitch the wounds and test Panther with his stethoscope.

M. *[As Dr Seal]* 'I'll have to take his heart out.' *[He cuts it out and holds it up to examine it.]*

I am struck by the power of this image. It re-connects me with the strong body language of both Mark and his father when the question of their longing to be 'mates' again was raised at the beginning of this session. I want to give this image time to work, but I don't want to push the therapy down a path unduly shaped by my impressions. I'll simply hold it for a while by reacting, in my play, to its importance.

B. 'Oh . . . that sounds serious. . . . His heart?'

M. *[Examining it carefully]* 'It's all right. It can go back.'

B. 'I'm glad about that. I'm glad his *heart* isn't damaged.'

B's voice expresses relief, and an acknowledgment that an opposite outcome had been on the cards. The image is significant, not only in terms of Mark's feeling that he could have died when his father attacked him, but also in terms of his desire for closeness with his father.

   Mark makes Dr Seal go off, his work completed.

B. 'Panther will need someone to be with him. Whom shall we get?'

Mark chooses a large, soft koala and puts him right beside Panther near the foot of the bed. He strokes Panther with Koala's large soft paws.

B. *[Doubling]* 'Oh, that feels good! . . . Thank you!'

Koala continues to stroke. B joins in, using her hands to express the feeling Mark is displaying. There is an atmosphere of great tenderness. Mark then jumps up and brings a small kangaroo to the bed.

M. 'He needs you too.' *[Placing Kangaroo on Panther's chest]*

B. 'Who is that?'

M. 'That's a friend.'

B. 'Very good. . . . He needs friends.'

She stays there with Mark while he strokes Panther. She doubles for him, using his gestures, extending them, maximizing the tenderness. There is total peace. Perhaps the time has come when Mark can engage in a new way with his father's role in this whole situation.

B. 'I'm not sure about this, but I'm wondering . . . just wondering . . . if we should try to talk to the person who did this thing? . . . Shall we?'

Mark nods. B clears the stage, leaving a free space for this new scene.

B. 'Choose something to be him.'

Mark examines the toys in the cupboard carefully. He chooses the punk doll with spiky purple hair and a safety pin in his ear. He immediately reverts to a frenzy of bashing, throwing, kicking, stomping.

B. *[Doubling with groans, cries, pleadings, wincing, screaming. Finally she stands up, as director, and says]* 'This man needs help. Stop! Get someone to help him.'

Mark continues for some time, enjoying the role, then picks up the punk doll, looks at it reflectively and says: 'It's all right. . . . It's finished now.' *He puts the punk doll back into the cupboard, then goes over to the door, peering through the stained glass section of the door, out into the darkness of the garden.*

M. 'Is Dad out there?'

B. 'Yes, somewhere.'

M. 'Let's get him to play too. . . . Have you got a torch?'

B gives him one and he sets off among the tea-trees, enjoying the light on the garden.

B, as director, has to decide on the next step. She knows Mark has reached a climax that has led to peace. There is no point in re-tracing the steps. Also, his request for a torch to help him find his Dad in the dark is metaphorically perfect for what he now wants to do. And it is also metaphorically perfect for his father's whole intention in co-operating with the therapy.

She decides to focus on their need to learn new patterns of communicating, so when they re-enter the room, she invites them both to draw a picture of some happy time in their life together. They do this separately. When they come to look at each other's drawings, Mark demonstrates infantile, counter-productive be-haviour as he communicates by shouting, ridiculing his father's picture, jumping around, playing aggressively and rudely to-wards his Dad with a large monkey puppet. He resists all B's attempts to engage him differently. It looks like a display of an old habit, a form of baiting this inarticulate man to notice him, to relate to him.

B. *[To Monkey]* 'Come here, Jimmy.'
   [To Mark] 'Give him to me.'
B interacts gently, firmly, lovingly with the monkey.
   'Now just come here. . . . Sit there now. . . . That's the boy. . . . That's much better.'
She strokes the monkey, and cuddles him on her shoulder for a minute.
   'Now . . . sit down here. Right beside Mark. And drop this silly stuff. . . . We're going to ask Mark's Dad to tell us about his drawing. And we're going to listen to him. We might even learn something about him if we do. . . . That's what we're here for tonight, Mark, isn't it?'
Mark's eyes register. B has scored a bull's eye. He is interested in being reached so deeply. He does not have to try to be receptive. He just is.

The session drew to a close with some good interaction and some good discussion, touching on the fact that they both had ferocious tempers, and that they did not really know how to talk with each other. I met them several more times, and later sessions focussed on Mark's concept of his own 'badness'. Sadly, the work was interrupted when Mark's family had to move to a distant country town. But he had engaged with his problem so fully through the medium of this shared play that the insights had probably become absorbed at a deep enough level to endure.

In one hour, Mark taught me more than weeks of reading would have done. In the moment of interrupting his cathartic experience of the role of the aggressor, I was exploring a new path. The thoughts that moved through my mind (at the lightning speed the situation required) were in line with some reading I did a few years later. I came upon a monograph by Moreno and his wife, in which they discussed the power and limitations of play with dolls. They described dolls as

> Beings who can be loved and hated in excess, and who cannot love or fight back, who can be destroyed without murmur, in other words, dolls are like individuals who have lost their spontaneity.
>
> (Moreno and Moreno 1944:29)

At the time of my session with Mark, I wanted to help him explore the victim role as well as the role of aggressor, and I wanted him to discover the person of the aggressor. The exploration of the freedom of untrammelled rage was part of that, but only a part. To let him project that rage on to an unresisting doll, and to leave it at that, would have been to leave him with his own confused feelings.

I knew that a child as young as Mark could not handle role-reversal in the form that is used in adult psychodrama, but I decided to experiment with a form of doubling, using the puppet, as a way of leading him to identify with the victim. He then showed what well-springs of tenderness this opened up, and so I followed his play with more confidence, knowing that together we could unfold this whole experience, in a far more valuable way than unrestrained catharsis would have allowed. Mark became one of many children on my list of memorable teachers.

10

JODY

Like Mark, Jody went straight into self-directed, healing play. The metaphors were equally strong, though her style was simpler. She was only three years old. Her closest playmate had been run over by a car when she suddenly ran on to the road to retrieve a ball. Several children were present, but Jody was the only one who actually saw the wheels go over her little playmate's head. She heard it crack. Her behaviour since the accident had been wildly hyperactive and her parents brought her to me for help. She was unable to accept her friend's death and kept talking as if she expected her to come and play.

FIRST SESSION

In the free play section of the session, Jody heads straight for a large Humpty Dumpty, a toy that has been universally neglected until now. She is striding around, stamping her feet, and frequently saying 'Jah, Jah', as she drags out Humpty Dumpty and places him on the back of a chair. I realize she has taken the lead and that she has instinctively chosen a puppet that has enormous metaphorical significance for her. We are entering a full-scale therapeutic session. It is for me to follow her. I will only introduce new elements to the game if an opportunity arises to deepen her own exploration. There is no need at present to do anything except to move alongside her play in an unobtrusive and supportive fashion. I softly sing the nursery rhyme as she lines up 'All the King's horses and all the King's men' – a King, a Queen, a Princess, an Arab on a camel, and a bejewelled Afghan horse. When Humpty Dumpty falls, he is put together again and returned to the chair top.

B. 'There you are, Humpty Dumpty, stay there now.' [*This is in response to Jody's emphatic, determined placement of him.*]
Jody keeps talking to herself, incoherently on the whole, as she moves busily around, arranging the toys the way she wants them. Her body movements are very, very resolute. It is as though I am hardly present to her.

IN THE SECOND SESSION

Jody begins to introduce elements of the accident into the story. When Humpty Dumpty falls and I give a startled cry, she shouts 'Don't touch! Don't touch! Too much blood!'

B. [*Maximizing this, stands over Humpty Dumpty, shaking her hands free of blood shuddering and saying distractedly*] 'Oh! . . . Oh! . . . Too much blood! . . . Too much blood!'
B recognizes the crucial significance of this sudden intrusion of real-life material into the play. Doubling for the child, she has entered into something of the horror of the original experience. Jody moves on matter-of-factly. Humpty Dumpty is put together yet again and warned to remember what his mother said about staying on the wall.

IN THE THIRD SESSION

In the period between sessions, there has been a growth in Jody's ability to explore her reaction to the trauma. When Humpty Dumpty falls, Jody shouts, 'All the children inside! Quickly, quickly! All the children inside!'

B rushes to gather armfuls of toys from around the room, speeding them into cupboards and slamming the doors. Jody joins her in this frenetic activity.
B. 'Quickly! Quickly! All the children inside!'
J. 'Too much blood! Too much blood!'
B. [*Shudders and agrees.*] 'TOO much blood.'
As before, Jody makes Humpty Dumpty return to his place on the wall.

IN THE FOURTH SESSION

We re-enact all this, following Jody's initiatives all the time. But today, she suddenly stops her rushing, busy play to say 'Can't mend him . . . no good. . . .'

B. 'Oh! . . . Can't **mend** him? . . . What shall we do?'
J. [*Matter-of-factly*] 'We'll bury him.'
B. 'Can you do that?'
J. 'Yes.'
B. 'Where shall we bury him?'
J. 'Here.'
She thumps him down on the door mat, and makes fluttering, busy, patting movements with her hands a few centimetres above his body.
B. 'Shall we say good-bye to Humpty Dumpty?'
We do that. B goes on to maximize the tenderness of this scene, but retaining the child's simplicity of words and gestures.
B. 'Let's be the sun, shining down on Humpty Dumpty.'
We do that, and Jody abruptly ends the game. She mentions her friend, just passingly, and the next day asks her parents to take her to the cemetery.

From then on, Jody's hyperactivity simmered down and she spoke of her friend in ways that acknowledged she would not be coming back.

Her parents told me she did not need to come for therapy any more. 'She's fixed *herself* really', they said. 'She just played "accident" games with the other children. And now she knows Megan's not coming back. She's fixed herself.'

11

JASON

Like many other fifteen-year-old boys I have known, Jason was not skilled in the art of problem-solving through words. He had run away from home more than once, and had also run away from the family-group home where he was now living with Joe and Rhonda as his principal care-givers. For some months, I had worked with him, building up his self-esteem and helping him to recognize his strengths as well as some of the mannerisms that were blocking his ability to make friends. He had visibly expanded within himself, and life opportunities were expanding for him too. It was very surprising to find his old running-away pattern re-emerging.

I decided to focus the session, initially, on my need to understand what goes on in him when he runs away. In the language of psychodrama, some 'social investigation' was necessary. When a director is unsure of what is happening internally for the protagonist at some crucial point in the production of a drama, she needs to investigate. This can be done by questioning. (In Jason's case, this would have resulted in answers like: 'Yes', 'No', or 'I dunno'.) Another way is by scene-setting.

The following account of the session shows how a form of scene-setting was used, with puppets being placed to form a picture of the running-away event. As I worked with him, I mentally noted roles that emerged: extrovert, cocky bragster; disguised mouse; directionless, drifting victim. The latter role was central to his problems. I decided to draw it out, making it visible to Jason – first with words that teased out the various strands in his particular form of victim behaviour, and then by using a fragile, floppy-necked little monkey puppet to concretize the ideas. The session began with my original wish to understand,

and then opened out to explore the issues his picture revealed.

Jason sits down in his usual non-committal way,

B. 'How've you been?'

J. 'Good.'

B. 'How's life?'

J. 'Good.'

B. 'Didn't sound too good from what Rhonda told me. She said you'd run away.'

J. 'Yeah.'

B. 'I was a bit surprised. Things seemed to have been going well for you.'

J. *[Sits with a blank, vacuous expression, nodding].* 'The CSV people said they'd probably put me in a hostel next time I run away.'

B. 'WHAT!!! "Next time you run away?" So it's taken for granted you're going to do it again. You take it for granted! They take it for granted! . . . Well . . . I **don't!**'

Jason looks a bit startled, but waits for what comes next from this unpredictable therapist.

B. 'Let's have a look at what goes on in you when you run away . . . I don't really know what it's like for you . . . I try to imagine it, and maybe I guess right sometimes. But maybe I'm wrong . . . I sometimes think it must be exciting and I sometimes think it must be scary. . . . And I wonder if you're angry, or if you're sad and lonely. . . . How about you show me what it was like this time? Let's set it up like a picture. Tell me about it. What started the idea off?'

J. 'Well, Mike said he was gonna run away and he said would I come too.'

B. 'Okay. Choose something to be Mike and something to be you.'

Jason does this.

B. 'Where are you?'

J. 'We're in a train.'

B. 'Make the train. Put Jason and Mike where they are in the train.'

Jason does this.

B. 'Is there anyone else in this story?'

J. 'There's a guy sitting behind us.'

B. 'Put him there. . . . Is there anyone else?'

J. 'No.'
B. 'I think there are some other people you're not thinking about. You probably didn't think about them then either.'
Jason looks puzzled.
B. 'Aren't there some grown-ups who might be worried?'
Jason looks interested.
B. 'Did you give a thought to any of them?'
J. [*Nods.*] 'Mike's mum. And his sister.'
B. 'Where are they?'
J. 'At home.'
B. 'Put them there. . . . I'm afraid you'll just have to stay there with your worries. These boys aren't really giving you much thought at the moment.' [*To Jason*] 'Anyone else?'
J. [*Shakes head*] 'No.'
B. 'Choose something to be Rhonda and Joe.'
Jason gives an 'Oh, gosh, I forgot them' sort of look and chooses some puppets.
B. 'Well, you'll have to go here, **right** out of sight.' [*She puts them in a closed section of the cupboard.*] 'Jason's not sparing even half a thought to you at the moment. He's all caught up in whatever it is that goes on in him when he's running away.' [*To Jason*] 'Let's get back to these characters in the train. . . . What's happening with them? Go over there and be Jason.'
Jason picks up puppet representing him.
B. 'Well, what's happening?'
J. 'We're talking and laughing and having some smokes.'
B. 'What are you talking about?'
J. 'About what station we'll get off at, and where we'll go. And we're talking about Refuges and where you can get food vouchers and stuff.'
B. 'And where will you go?'
J. 'We don't know. We'll just see what turns up.'
B. 'So . . . you're laughing as you talk. And you're smoking and looking as though you're in the big time . . . and that's on the top. . . . Is it the same with your feelings underneath?'
Jason reflects for a minute.
J. 'I'm a bit scared. I don't know what will happen. We'll end up getting into trouble.'
B. 'But right now no-one would know that by looking at you. You're rocking in the train with your mates, talking, laughing, smoking. . . . So, go on with the story. What happens then?'

J. 'Well, this guy's been looking at me. And he starts talking to us.'

B. 'What does he say?'

J. 'Well, he just joins in. We're talking about music we like. . . . And then he finds out we're running away. . . . And he says we can go to his place.'

B. 'And you do?'

Jason nods.

B. 'Make that happen.'

Jason takes the puppets off the train. He sets up a corner to represent the house.

B. 'Is there anyone else in this house?'

J. 'Yes. His mum.'

B. 'Choose something to be his mum. . . . Show me what happens then.'

J. 'Well . . . she gives us some food and then she says we can stay the night.' [*He enacts this.*]

B. 'Hmm . . . quite an adventure . . . everyone really looking after you. So you settle down to sleep in this strange house. This running away is turning out all right for the moment . . . and you're just following what happens, moment by moment.'

Jason nods.

B. 'So, you slept well?'

Jason nods.

B. 'Morning comes . . . then what?'

J. 'Well, the lady gave us some breakfast. Then she got the cops to come to take us home.'

B. 'M'm . . . that's a new twist to the story. . . . Or maybe it's not. . . . In a way, it means you were lucky for the second time.'

Jason looks puzzled.

B. 'You're being rescued again. The first time was when the young guy in the train took you home to an old-fashioned mum who was into looking after kids. If he'd been a different sort of character you could have ended up in big trouble. . . . We've talked about this before. Last time you ran away. . . . '

Jason nods.

B. 'Anyway, here you are again. Luckily, you're safe and well fed and warm and with friendly people. And this lady wants the cops to take you back to somewhere safe. . . . Choose something to be the policeman.'

Jason chooses Paddington Bear.

B. 'Yes. You'll do. You seem to have quite an impressive uniform.' *[To J]* But there's something I've been thinking all the time you've been setting up this picture for me. I've been seeing something else. Something that's under the surface of this story.... Come out here.' *[To the floppy baby monkey]* 'I need you to help me show Jason what I see.' *[She holds the monkey by the scruff of the neck, making him flop helplessly wherever she chooses to swing him or make him drift.]* 'This is Jason, when he's in the role of "Victim". Do you know what I mean by "victim"?'

Jason shakes his head.

B. 'A victim kind of person goes through life just taking what comes, letting other people decide what will happen to him. And when it's good, he goes along with that. If it's bad, he doesn't know how to get out of his troubles. It's as if he's cast adrift on the sea. Maybe the sea will dash him against the rocks. Maybe the sea will wash him up on soft sand. ...'

B moves the puppet as if it is being tossed around by the sea.

'That's how it was for you in this running-away episode. Mike says: "I'm running away. Will you come?" And you come. The guy in the train says "Come to my place" and you come. That young man could easily have been one of those people you know very well hang around our railway stations. You could have been washed up on the rocks of sexual abuse. ... But this story ended up with you flopping on the soft sand of the "rescuer's" world. ... That's how it is with victims. They're always ending up either persecuted or rescued. Someone else is always in charge. They don't have any say in how their lives will go.'

Jason is watching the little monkey's helpless floating with a look of growing concentration. His face reflects that he sees this as an accurate picture of himself and he doesn't like what he sees.

B. 'Now, there's something a bit wrong with this picture I'm creating here. ... It's only half the picture, it's only one side of your nature. We've often talked about the strong side of yourself – that has helped you grow up so much these past few months. You've learned to hold yourself straight, look people in the eye when you talk to them, make new friends, open that gate in the wall you've built around yourself when life's been hard. That Jason has a lot of strength. Choose something to be him.'

Jason chooses a colourful lion, dressed as a king.

B. 'Good choice!' *[To the lion]* 'Yes, you'll do nicely to show the strong side of Jason. I like your crown. You're a king. You're not made to be pushed around by life – drifting here, drifting there. Come over here, the two of you, and be with Jason who's in the act of being rescued by the policeman.' *[She brings them over to the puppet already chosen by J to represent himself.]* . . . *[To J]* 'Right . . . so the policeman brings you back. Mike to his mum and his sister' *[She re-unites the puppets representing them.]* 'and you to Rhonda and Joe. Now, in this room, we don't have to show everything exactly the way it really was at the time. I can see by your face that you've been doing quite a bit of thinking while you and I have made these pictures for each other. Has this new, thinking Jason got anything to say to Rhonda and Joe?'

J. *[Thinks for a while.]* 'I'm sorry you've been worried. I forgot about you.'

B. 'Well, I'm sure they appreciate that. It's good to hear you say it. . . . Now, before we finish up, is there anyone else here that you want to say something to?'

J. *[Looks for a while at the array of puppets. He picks up the little monkey and hurls it away.]* 'I don't want you! I don't want to be a victim!'

B. *[Retrieves the monkey, holding him tenderly.]* 'Well, he can't be got rid of quite so easily. He's there because some really hurtful things have happened in your life. You've been hurt very deeply. And up until now, you haven't known how else to cope when things go wrong. But you're learning – more and more every day – that there's a strong side to you as well.' *[She moves the lion over, getting him to hold the monkey.]* *[To the lion]* 'So, look after this little bloke, will you? . . . And when he gets caught up with wanting to go back to old ways of coping, keep him there with you.' *[To J]* 'It's time for us to finish now. So place these puppets that represent you in a way that makes a good ending to the work we've done today.'

Jason moves them together to a shelf high up in the room with the lion in central top position and looks at them thoughtfully.

B. *[Nods in appreciation.]* 'Good! . . . Now let's put them all away.

They've worked well with us today. Who knows what children will choose them for another story tomorrow.'

Jason followed up these insights with some unexpected and very strong decision-making. By the time he came for his next session, a few weeks later, he had initiated a re-union with his estranged family, spending a day with them. He later arranged to be part of an extended family gathering, and, interestingly, asked that his 'work experience' placement from school should be at his father's workplace, with his father as his boss. They were initiatives that did not turn out entirely as he had hoped, but in a later session he revealed considerable maturity in his handling of these disappointments. In his final session with me, he created a sculpture of his life at the present moment. Right at the top of his arrangement of the puppets was the kingly lion. He represented Jason's new-found ability not to let his family's rejection of him swamp his whole life. The rest of his sculpture showed the positive, enjoyable things that had developed for him. These were the areas of life he wanted to expand. 'I want to get on with it', he said.

A therapist becomes part of a person's life for only a short time. Sometimes a contact remains, and occasional scraps of news give a hint of how that life later unfolds. But more often than not, the therapist must let go completely, knowing that others are involved in the ongoing healing process or in its obstruction. Jason has remained in my consciousness as a boy for whom I knew the future held many question marks. The child-care agency responsible for his placement in the cottage home did not work with young people over the age of sixteen. At this time there had been changes to the legislation through the Children and Young Persons Act of 1989, many of them aimed at further reducing the institutionalization of young people. Those in care were encouraged to move into independent living at the age of sixteen, where this seemed appropriate. Jason wanted to stretch his wings and he moved into a private house with a group of young friends. There were quite significant changes occurring in the protective services system at the time.

The gradual implementation of the Act, from 1989 to 1993, brought in a period of reform, with statutory and voluntary organizations having to adjust to a different style of partnership aimed at deflecting adolescents from unnecessary involvement with the system. Fogarty (1993:33) accused the government of having abnegated responsibility for these young people. And there were, indeed, gaps in the services provided for them. More probably, however, the gaps were connected with a failure adequately to plan the practical aspects of change *ahead* of the promulgation of the Act. That, at least, was the initial impression of many in the voluntary sector. It took time for a more effective collaboration to occur between the government and the community it wanted to engage. So Jason was branching out into independent living at a time when support services were in a state of flux.

Many details of Jason's life have been omitted here, to protect his identity. I tried to contact him to discuss the place his story holds in this book, but could find only the faintest traces of his path since he turned sixteen. It may be that he survived well, glad to explore the world in independence. My knowledge of his earlier brushes with the hard facts of life leaves me wondering how any boy of his age could survive strongly with so flimsy a caring network around him. But then I remind myself of the unusual strength with which he followed through the insights he gained when I knew him. Perhaps he will retain this ability, making use of even the smallest opportunities life has to offer him.

It is beyond the scope of this book to research the situation in the United Kingdom and the USA. They, too, have had governments that subscribed to the theories of the economic rationalists – the trend-setters of the 1980s and 1990s – with their emphasis on the market economy as the central plank in policy formation. Emy and Hughes (1988) sum up the mood:

> The concept of the market economy ... suggests that basic conflicts over resources – over who gets what, when and how – can really be handled better by the impersonal economic institutions of the market than by government. . . . 'Let the market decide' is a political as well as a purely economic statement.
>
> (Emy and Hughes 1988:116)

Under governments steered by this philosophy, the policy-makers in the field of welfare have emphasized the need to measure results in terms of economic efficiency. Some would argue that there is, at this stage, a tendency to over-emphasize such a need, and to use what Fogarty (1993:31) calls 'budget-driven planning'. Appearing before the 1992 US Senate Committee on Juvenile Justice, speaker after speaker referred to the need for a more global view in budget allocation and framing of preventative services for juveniles – with well-designed programmes being given *consistent* and *adequate* funding on a pro-active rather than a re-active basis. Martinez (1992) noted the first signs of a move away from the 'bleeding-heart social fixers' label for those who plead the case for needy children and their families. She applauds this trend and calls for a stronger sense of society's future: 'we have to stop thinking of investment in children as a give-away program and begin to recognize it as the real investment process that it is' (Martinez 1992:38).

Early help for a child struggling with emotional problems or caught in a social trap pays dividends that prevent escalating disfunction later. Even the economic rationalists should understand that. But they appear (at least in Australia) to base their arguments on statistics that measure (to borrow the current ministerial jargon) such things as 'through-put' – i.e. the numbers of children and young persons being served by an agency in a given period. There are no statistics quoted that attempt to measure 'who has been put through what' in the process, and so the statistics are unreliable indicators of how well the needs of troubled children are being met.

Jason's unfinished story is but one of those that illustrate the impact on children's lives of the wider social system. The above discussion of budget-driven planning (so prevalent in the profit-conscious world of the 1980s and 1990s) is limited both by the nature of this book and by the dearth of appropriate statistics. The effects of economic rationalism on the delivery of well-planned, well-coordinated and appropriate services for children and young people at risk is a question for future research. It needs to be pursued.

12

MARY KATE

Mary Kate's grandfather had been sexually abusing her severely for five years (when she was aged between three and eight). Her mother realized what was happening one evening when they had gone to visit Mary Kate's grandmother. Mary Kate remained in the lounge room with her grandfather while her mother went into the bedroom. A strange look on the face of the dog alerted the mother when she returned to the lounge room. She confronted her father. (He had abused her as a child, and later it became clear he had also abused other family members.) In the events that followed, the extended family put Mary Kate's family into virtual 'Coventry'. Her previous therapist Sandra had helped her with the earliest post-disclosure period, but she was no longer working at the agency.

Towards the end of my second session with Mary Kate, her mother suggested one of my dolls looked like a grandmother. I asked Mary Kate if she had a grandmother. A shadow passed over her face. She looked at her mother, as if asking for complicity, and said, 'She's dead'. I decided to pass over this at the time and to follow it up in our next therapy session.

THE THIRD SESSION

Today I have decided to follow the unusual path of self-disclosure to help Mary Kate have the courage to allow another person to lead her in exploring the issue of abandonment. This child's defences are strong, and I have been asked to work with her for a very limited period only. I will take a risk in tapping on the walls of her need to deny. If she is able to let me in, I will follow where she leads.

Mary Kate, as usual, has gone straight into exploratory play with the toys. Before her mother leaves, I begin:

B. 'I've been thinking about you a lot lately. Last time you came, I could see your heart was hurting. You told me your grandmother was dead. I knew about her. Your mum had told me. And I saw in your eyes that your heart was hurting, badly. . . . Something happened in my life once that hurt so badly I wished I could die. A whole lot of people I had cared about just didn't want to know me any more. I knew I wouldn't die, but sometimes I wished I could just puff out. I thought I had to be brave, so I pushed it down and pretended I was okay. But it kept coming up to the surface at the most unexpected times, so, in the end, I decided to go and see someone who works the way I do. Someone who could help me look at my troubles and find out what to do about them. And while I'm telling you this, I see your eyes; they're warm, and soft, and brown, and they're telling me you understand. . . . Do you see this little dog?'

B hands Mary Kate a little soft-toy dog with floppy ears and no eyes. Mary Kate handles it with interest.

'Another little girl I worked with gave that to me. She thought it might be useful for some other child. See . . . it has no eyes. . . . This little girl was a bit like you when I first met her.'

B mirrors Mary Kate when she's in a cover-up mood, smiling brightly and falsely.

'She was afraid to look her troubles in the eye, so she kept pretending they weren't there. But gradually, we made up games and stories about them, and she learned to understand them better. You know, there are lots of children in a situation like yours, children who've been sexually abused. And quite often their families don't back them up when they speak out about it. I wonder about that . . . and I get very angry, and I wonder why they do it.'

M.K. 'Sandra said it's because families take sides and then they split up.'

B. 'Yes. That's part of it. And I think it might also be because grown-ups find it very hard to look this thing in the eye. They see it as very wrong for an older person to do sexual things with a little child. When two little children do sexual things together (like ordinary touching of each other or looking at parts of each other's bodies), it can feel okay for them, and it's

90

natural, and it fits with what they know. But when a grown-up does it, he knows different things a child hasn't had time to learn yet. And his body is bigger. And the child gets hurt and muddled up in her feelings. So grown-ups don't like to think of someone they know doing this to a little child, hurting her, and confusing her, and making her live in a land of secrets . . . so they won't look.'

B makes the dog's floppy ears cover the space where the eyes should be.
    'And if they stop seeing the child, they can let themselves forget. Maybe that's part of what's happening for them.'

Mary Kate listens thoughtfully to all this, looking at B intently. In the silence that follows, she gives some small, slow nods and a long sigh.

As the session continues, she becomes increasingly confident and open. She displays a natural talent as a story-maker, and B follows this, adding to the story only when she sees a way to assist Mary Kate to develop parallels with her own situation. Mary Kate moves in and out of reality as she creates the story, and B moves with her. This is an unusual form of therapeutic storytelling, but it is the way that opens out naturally with Mary Kate.

B.   'So, when Mum goes and leaves us to play, maybe we could make up a story about this little dog. We'll make it a bit like your story, but different wherever we want it to be. Let's see what story comes.'

Mary Kate readily lets her mind open to this and her mother leaves us together.

M.K. 'Once upon a time, there was a little dog called . . . Minnie.'

She stops here, so B helps her decide on Minnie's problem. They finally come up with the idea that 'Meaney Mick', a rather strange-looking monkey in work-overalls, has been pulling out Minnie's claws.

B.   'Minnie tried to hide her poor damaged little paws, and no-one knew what was happening.' [In an aside to M.K.] 'Let's see if we can get someone into the story who's a bit like Gran.'

M.K. 'One day she tried to tell her friend.'

She chooses the pink doll, whose mouth is set in a tight, permanent smile, and whose clothes and hair-do are very prim and correct.

B.   'What's her name?'

M.K. 'Pollyanna.'

B.   [Laughs] 'That's a perfect name for her. Do you know about the storybook character called Pollyanna?'

Mary Kate shakes her head.

B. 'Well, Pollyanna was a girl who thought the best way to deal
with troubles was to step around them and play the Glad
Game. It's quite a good idea to look for things to be glad about
when you're unhappy, but if you overdo it, you end up not
looking your troubles in the eye. I think maybe your Gran is
wanting to be a bit like Pollyanna at the moment.'

*Mary Kate smiles and continues with the story. She's good at this col-
laborative form of story-making.*

M.K. ' "Please listen to me", said Minnie.'

B. 'But Pollyanna didn't want to know. She ran and hid behind a
fan.'

*Mary Kate looked sad here and was a bit stumped in continuing with the
story. So B brought in some characters that would help Mary Kate tap
into her own inner wisdom.*

B. 'Tinkerbelle saw what was happening, and she saw that
Minnie was upset and didn't know what to do. So she flew off
to get Wise Owl.'

*Mary Kate helps B to create Owl sleeping in a high tree, and then flying
back with Tinkerbelle to where Pollyanna is hiding.*

B. 'Then Owl waved a wand to reach Pollyanna in that secret
place in her heart where wisdom is kept. Pollyanna listened as
Tinkerbelle encouraged her to come out from behind the fan.
"There's good and bad in the world", said Tink. "It's okay to
look. No harm will come to you." '

M.K. *[As Pollyanna]* 'All right . . . but I'm running straight back if
it's anything bad!'

B. 'So Tinkerbelle and Minnie both told Pollyanna what Meaney
Mick did.'

M.K. 'And said.'

B. 'Yes. That's important.'

*Mary Kate has stepped outside her role as storyteller for a moment. She's
talking to me directly, reminding me of an important aspect of her real
life story. I join her in the real world for a moment and ask 'What did Pa
say?'*

M.K. ' "They won't believe you. They'll laugh at you. They know I
wouldn't hurt you." And I thought: "What? You ARE hurting
me!" '

B nods, her face expressing empathy.

B. 'And that made you get all confused, and very muddled up in
your feelings, and scared. So . . . what happens next in our story?'

M.K. 'Pollyanna listened. Then she went straight to Meaney Mick. "What have you been doing to Minnie?" she said.'

B. *[Aside to M.K.]* 'How does Meaney Mick feel about this?'

M.K. 'He's glad. He wants to come out. He wants to tell.'

B. *[Maximizing]* 'Good! That's very good, Meaney Mick! Come on out. Come right out! And *tell*! Come on, come on out, Meaney Mick! And *tell*!'

Mary Kate responds with energy. She has now entered fully into the psychodramatic play.

M.K. 'So Meaney Mick comes out and tells Pollyanna what he has done. And they told all Minnie's friends.'

B. 'Gather the friends together. Gather them round. Come on everybody! Gather round. Come and hear!'

Mary Kate busily runs around, gathering a collection of small puppets: Slippery Sam, the penguin; Strawberry Shortcake, the mouse; Roo; Owl; Hedgehog; Little Red Riding Hood.

M.K. 'And Meaney Mick stood there while Pollyanna told all Minnie's friends. Then Minnie and Tinkerbelle went to the police. The policeman listened.'

She puts the police helmet on Panther and has him sitting in a chair, nodding as he listens.

M.K. 'The policeman took Meaney Mick to the police station to get a statement. They put him in gaol.'

Mary Kate's mouth is set in a hard, determined line, as she plonks Meaney Mick down and moves around him in a rectangular space, clanging down the bars.

M.K. *[Triumphantly, and finishing with a huge smile in B's direction]* 'And they threw away the key!!'

B shares the smile. She spends time with Mary Kate celebrating her triumph, dancing around the gaol, shouting 'Hooray!'. She then goes on to talk with Mary Kate about the key of secrecy that had locked her in prison too.

B. 'You're learning to throw away the key, through our games and through our talking.'

B looks at Mary Kate's face, radiant with release. She looks out of the french windows to the spring garden and calls Mary Kate to look too.

B. 'The garden is just like your face right now, lit up by sunshine, with the wind sweeping the world to freshness, and with flowers everywhere. Let's bring the garden in here.'

She flies over to the case where the scarves are kept, and whirls around with Mary Kate, creating beautiful beds of flowers and opening umbrellas of flowering trees. They each take a golden yellow scarf and dance round the room as the sun, shining into all the dark and secret places, as B shouts

B. 'Come out! Come out! All Mary Kate's fears! All Mary Kate's sadness! Come out, and let us shine on you!'

Turning to Mary Kate, and mirroring the radiance of her upturned face, B continues with gentleness and love in her voice.

'And the sun shone down on them, and the wind blew them far away. And the flowers in Mary Kate's heart turned radiant, smiling faces to the sun as they opened, one,

by one,

by one,

by one.'

SOME CELEBRATIONS

For Mary Kate's final session, we had a celebration of all the themes she'd covered in the past few months:

Mary Kate learns to come out from behind the fan   Mary Kate chose to re-enact the scene of the disclosure of her problem again. This turned into a celebration of the part her mother had played in stopping 'all the yukkie things'. Together, we ended up prancing and dancing around the room singing (tune courtesy Gilbert and Sullivan):

> Give three cheers and one cheer more
> For Marlene Reardon who stopped it all!
> Give three cheers for the dog who saw
> And . . . for . . . Marlene . . . who stopped it all!

B. 'Three cheers for Mary Kate's mum!! Hip, hip,'
B. & M.K. 'Hooray!'
B. 'Hip, hip,'
B. & M.K. 'Hooray!!'
B. 'Hip, hip,'
B. & M.K. *[With great gusto]* 'HOORAY!!!'

Marlene is present for this session. She is visibly moved by Mary Kate's expression of appreciation. She has had to cope with many painful memories of her own as she has backed Mary Kate during the past ten months. It has been exceedingly difficult.

We also celebrated other themes, one of the most liberating being 'The Rage'. At the beginning of the session, I had invited Mary Kate to help me set up a series of tableaux around the room, representing significant therapy sessions. There was one in which a large cushion had been draped with some red cloth.

B.   'What next?'

M.K. 'Let's do "The Rage"'

Her eyes sparkled with enjoyment as she remembered the day I encouraged her to reveal the feelings behind a massive explosion of temper at home. She had gone to her room after a minor remonstrance from her mother and hurled all her toys and all her beloved books at the walls, leaving a few holes and much chaos. She had come to therapy, smiling as sweetly as ever, and saying she'd had a good week. A re-enactment of the temper tantrum (which her mother had told me about) was very cathartic and had led us both to discover the real cause of her strong feelings.

B.   Sharing her enjoyment: 'Yes! Let's do "The Rage"!'

She strides around the room, doubling for Mary Kate, and waving the red cloth.

B.   'Mary Kate is in a RAGE! In fact, it could be said, Mary Kate Reardon is in a RIGHT, ROYAL RAGE! And what's more, she has a right to be.'

B.   *[To M.K.]* 'Get up there, Mary Kate Reardon' *[pointing to a table]* 'and tell the universe WHY you have a right to be in a rage!'

B runs to the other end of room, turns to face Mary Kate, who is beaming at her from the table-top.

B.   'Tell the mountains, and the rivers, and the sea and the sky; tell the sun and the moon; tell every star; tell the birds and the flowers, and every living thing WHY you have a right to be in a rage!'

M.K. *[Enjoying all this to the full, and speaking with great force.]* 'I'm in a rage! And I have a right to be! Because it's Grandparents' Day at school. All the other grandparents have come. And my Gran isn't there. So I can't be in it . . . and I had a right to be in it!!'

B.   'So, come on, Mary Kate. Let's celebrate the day you let the rage get out from your heart where you'd bottled it up.'

She gets Mary Kate quickly to set out the toys and the cushions representing the books.

B.   'Come on, be quick. Don't let it cool down! Let it out, Mary Kate, and let's see it!'

Mary Kate sits on the floor, hurling the soft toys and the cushions while B maximizes her actions, whirling around her, brandishing the red cloth.
B. 'So come on, Mary Kate!' [*And she tosses the red cloth to her.*]
   'Celebrate the day you admitted you were in a rage.'
Mary Kate does a marvellous, matador-like dance with the red cloth, finally keeping rhythm with B's shout,
   'Mary Kate Reardon . . . has a right to be angry . . . and she's letting it all OUT!!'
They both end up laughing, gathering up the toys, the cushions, the scarves, and each other.

In the thirteen weeks of our work together, Mary Kate moved a long way from presenting as a repressed, unhappy child with a prim, precise manner. She was quite startled the first time I leapt on to a table-top to create 'the mountain of truth' and invited her to join me there. But by the time we'd reached this final session, her body language was expressing far more freedom, mirroring the state of inner peace she had finally achieved. She had coped well with being interviewed by the police at the time of making her initial statement – partly because she had a facility with words and an ability to state facts simply and clearly; and partly because her mother was able to give her total support, having to go through the process herself in relation to her own long-buried abuse. The fact that her mother had come so close to actually witnessing one of grandfather's actions no doubt also helped to give the child credibility in the eyes of the police. And this was very probably a significant factor influencing her grandfather's decision to plead guilty when the time came for him to face trial.

In all this, she was more fortunate than many young victims of sexual abuse. She felt believed; she did not have to cope with the procedures in the court-room; and her simple, child-like understanding of justice matched the course of events. The system failed her at a later point, however, when the magistrate reviewing her claim for Victims of Crime Compensation refused to accept a report from a social worker. In order to win her claim she would have had to be assessed by an unknown psychologist and this would have meant re-living the trauma she had worked so hard to put behind her. Mary Kate (backed by her mother) refused to do this.

13

JAMIE

As Jamie's story moves into my mind, so too does this quotation from Hans Andersen's 'The Little Mermaid':

> Far out in the sea, the water is as blue as the petals of the loveliest of cornflowers, and as clear as the clearest glass; but it is very deep, deeper than any anchor-cable can reach, and many church towers would have to be put one on top of another to reach from the bottom out of the water.
>
> (James 1930:83)

A very young child who has experienced only love and nurturing care from his parents has an innocence and a trust in life that is as deep as the sea. An abuser can approach such a child (and the first approaches are usually made with care) secure in the knowledge that this child has not yet learnt the need for protective barriers. Survivors of long-term sexual abuse describe a process that characteristically involves a slow and gradual entrapment, with ensuing confusion, 'guilt' and paralysing fear of exposure, as the child victims are sucked in deeper and deeper.

If the child is as young as three (as was the case for both Mary Kate and Jamie) these tangled emotions are all the more confusing because, developmentally, the child is still moving out of a phase to which Moreno and Moreno (1944) give the name 'the first universe'.

> The first universe ends when the infantile experience of a world in which everything is real begins to break up into fantasy and reality. Image-building develops rapidly, and the differentiation between real and imagined things begins to take form.
>
> (Moreno and Moreno 1944:64)

The child moves fluidly between fantasy and reality and is very responsive to imagery at this stage. Sexual abusers of very young children often use toys and masks and other play equipment to introduce the sexual 'games'. This imagery is very vivid for the child and, as the entrapment progresses, the once simple toys become charged with metaphorical significance. The sight of similar play objects in quite another setting can bring a surge of memories affecting any one (or all) of the five senses. For children who have been deeply traumatized such flashbacks are felt in the present and there is a visible numbing of responsiveness with regard to their external world while this invasion of memories is occurring.

> It is as if time stops at the moment of trauma. The traumatic moment becomes encoded in an abnormal form of memory, which breaks spontaneously into consciousness, both as flashbacks during waking states and as traumatic nightmares during sleep. Small, seemingly insignificant reminders can also evoke these memories, which often return with all the vividness and emotional force of the original event. Thus, even normally safe environments may come to feel dangerous, for the survivor can never be assured that she will not encounter some reminder of the trauma.
>
> (Herman 1992:37)

For Jamie, in the ten months when I worked with him, this was a distressing part of life. His eyes would become huge, colour would drain completely from his face and he would be oblivious to his surroundings for several minutes. His whole body language would express the traumatic intensity of these memory flashbacks, and I knew that he was being affected at a very deep level of his being. Did I have an 'anchor cable' that could reach him? Or could I help him to build the many 'church towers', one on top of the other, that would reach up to me from the bottom of his extreme fear? He was a very intelligent, creative child and as we worked together I found that the sensitivity that had made him so vulnerable also worked for him as a healing mechanism.

Some sexual play with dolls had first alerted Jamie's parents to the possibility that their son (now four years old) had been abused. A short time later, Jamie disclosed a few details to his mother. The parents sought help through a Centre Against Sexual Assault, but Jamie was unable to talk directly to the counsellor. To his mother, over time, and using the language of a very young child, Jamie gradually revealed that his uncle had abused him severely, in the course of regular child-minding over a long period. This uncle was a trusted member of the extended family and a highly respected figure as a senior teacher at the local school. So his credibility rating was much higher than that of a four-year-old, unable to trust anyone but his mother. The police who attempted to interview Jamie on several occasions were unsuccessful in gaining his trust and they expressed scepticism that anything of significance had occurred.

According to the accounts I heard from his parents, when Jamie was later referred to me, the methods the police used showed little understanding of such a young child's response to trauma. They were a far cry from the effective teamwork Madge Bray (1991) describes in her story of Tracey, another very young child unable to cope with normal interviewing techniques (Bray 1991: 50–66). It is a wonderful account of a policeman following a play therapist's lead and trusting her not to interfere with the rules of evidence even while, together, they play exuberantly with a child, in a way that facilitates the otherwise terrifying process of obtaining a statement. How many children experience such understanding? Not enough. And how many can only make their disclosure after months of therapy, providing future barristers in court cases with the weapon of 'contaminated evidence' – an argument that implies the children are merely voicing the opinions of parents and therapists? Too many. Our legal system in its present form is a totally inadequate protector of very young victims of sexual abuse. Alice Miller, the noted psychiatrist, writes

Till now, society has protected the adult and blamed the victim. It has been abetted in its blindness by theories, still in keeping with the pedagogical principles of our great-grandparents, according to whom children are viewed as crafty creatures, dominated by wicked drives, who invent stories and attack their innocent parents or desire them sexually. In reality, children tend to blame themselves for their parents' cruelty and to absolve the parents, whom they invariably love, of all responsibility.

(Miller 1990:169)

In Jamie's case, the cruelty came from outside the nuclear family, but Miller's comments apply to the situation in general. The laws aimed at protecting children are still weighted more heavily in favour of adults because they are administered in settings that are more comprehensible to adults. Even though adults too are usually overawed by the unfamiliar language and the trappings of the legal system, they can engage with the legal process in a way that is far less possible for a child. The child needs massive help to cope.

Sandra Smith (1985), speaking within the framework of the United States system, gives many examples of how a prosecutor can assist a child to give evidence in such an alien setting. But she acknowledges that the increasing numbers of cases to hit the courts have resulted in increased sophistication in the defence (Smith 1985:54). In the introduction to her book, she sums up the child's position in the power equation as follows.

> David and Goliath was not history's first recorded one-on-one contest. Perhaps David *v.* Goliath has won historical recognition because of the disparity in the size and power of the participants. This same disparity is found in almost every case of child molestation. The most noticeable feature of this crime is the mismatch between offender and victim. The abuser is bigger, stronger, more experienced, better at verbal skills, and holds all the power in the relationship. The child-victim is small, weak, naive, inarticulate and powerless.
>
> (Smith 1985: Introduction)

When Jamie appeared on my doorstep, my task was not to help him fight a legal battle so much as to help him find healing. He was experiencing nightmares, was very afraid of strangers, had occasional outbursts of uncharacteristic aggression, and was going into trance-like states when memories of his abuse flooded his consciousness. The first six sessions followed Jamie's free play. He rapidly revealed himself as a child who could use metaphor and visual imagery to release emotion. I simply moved alongside his play as an auxiliary ego, taking on the roles he assigned to me and acting them out in ways that assisted him to explore his own roles more fully. At all times I took even more care than usual not to intrude any themes or interpretations of my own into the play. 'Contamination of the evidence' is anathema to any good therapist, and is scrupulously avoided in work with sexually abused children.

The themes Jamie introduced into his play included aggression, rage, revenge, deception, disaster, vulnerability, captivity. He often put me in the role of the 'baddie' – usually in the guise of Killer Whale, who was pursuing Little Seal. When, in my role as director, I would ask if there was anyone who could help Little Seal, he always readily produced protective figures. These characters would then fiercely pursue Killer Whale, and I would have to protect myself physically with cushions as Jamie hurled himself again and again at the aggressor now turned victim. I hammed up expressions of terror as he pursued me (to his great delight) and he took great pleasure in ignoring my desperate cries for help. The game had many different versions, and sometimes included deceptive figures – a gaily coloured cloth crocodile and a mild-faced baby monkey – that presented initially as friends but proved, in the end, to be enemies.

Another game, that was introduced several times over the ten months, had Humpty Dumpty as the main character. Moving away from the soft toy that had triggered his imagination, Jamie used two sea-urchin shells he found in my collection of beach-combing treasures. One represented Humpty Dumpty, the other his father, in protective role. He put them in a little boat and floated them in the bath, where a large container represented an island. A stone became the fox ('he can't swim') and a game of pursuit and accidents and final escape was enacted. Whenever Jamie played this game, he would have a noticeable physical reaction as fear was released – an almighty smell would fill the room and he would need a long and satisfying time in the toilet, from where he chatted to me quite happily about extraneous, everyday matters. The smell was less offensive each time this game was played.

But then a new development occurred. Jamie's mother overheard him discussing a possible suicide pact with his older sister. He appeared to be trying to work out a way for her to die first so that she would be in Heaven to meet him. She warned him that even if she jumped first, he might hit the ground before her. This incident alerted me to the needs of the older child. It was highly likely that she, too, was a victim of sexual abuse. In any case, she was carrying an enormous burden in being her little brother's confidante. I asked to see her also. And I decided to include a new element into the therapy to work alongside their free play. According to reports from the parents, both children were terrified that threats made by the abuser would be carried out, and their fear was being expressed so constantly and at times dramatically, that it seemed to me important to counterbalance these vivid images with messages of safety. We needed to reach them at the same depth (below that of rational cognition) that the abuser had targeted when he threatened their safety and that of their parents.

Bearing in mind the subliminal power of therapeutic storytelling, and avoiding even hints of sexual abuse, I developed, with each child, over the next few weeks a therapeutic story that paralleled themes occurring in his or her play but that included clear messages of safety. The stories were action-based and were illustrated with very graphic visual and kinetic imagery. They reinforced the message that the abuser's power to harm them had been cut off at its roots once Jamie freed himself from the secret-keeping which had previously given the abuser such power.

One such story told of the Moon (represented by a triangular-shaped paper lantern lit by a candle) shining down on Little Seal one night and observing his sleepless tossing and turning. She encouraged Little Seal to tell his mother what was worrying him, even though that meant telling on Killer Whale. (The story included details of Killer Whale's frightening games when he took Little Seal far out into the stormy seas to tease him – secretly, and with menacing threats of retaliation if Little Seal spoke up.) The Moon placed a cloak of courage on Little Seal's shoulders, and as he spoke it grew and grew. (We used a very long trail of beautifully coloured silken scarves that stretched right across the room.)

Meanwhile, Killer Whale was cruising, as usual, boasting of his power. (We attached a chicken-shaped balloon to Killer Whale's back. It emitted a piercing, squawking sound when squeezed, and it also had a little plug that could be pulled – making the sound disappear with a surprised gurgle, and reducing the puffed-up balloon to a scrap of limp rag.) When Little Seal spoke up, Killer Whale lost all his power (Jamie pulled the plug and laughed as Killer Whale's power visibly disintegrated). And all the flowers danced for joy (I turned a fan on to some flowers that rotated in the wind and they spun gaily, making a swirl of new colours). Jamie ran out into the garden, holding the flowers aloft to make them dance in the wind and I followed at full speed with

Little Seal, his cloak of courage streaming behind us. These images were developed by Jamie in later free play and by me in later storytelling, with the therapist always taking care to base them on mutually known data and never suggesting extra abuse-orientated facts or metaphors. For example, in the above story, Killer Whale's cruising was an allusion to the abuser's habit of making himself visible frequently, keeping the children's fear of his threats very active.

For Kelly, Jamie's sister, the central character that emerged in the stories was Penguin, Little Seal's friend. Penguin was carrying a huge bundle on his back. It was getting in the way of many things Penguin wanted to do, but he denied that it was there and didn't want anyone to come too close to see if it could be moved. He just went on with his life, staggering under the burden some-times, but acting as if there was nothing there. Kelly reacted when I began this story, hiding her face in some cushions and curling up away from me. Her free play strongly suggested that she had unusual depths of anger that needed to be released. On two occa-sions, just before a visit to me, she burst into tears when her mother picked her up from school. She always made an excuse for the tears – not very convincing ones – and said there was something in her throat that wouldn't let the words come out. At the time, I increasingly suspected that Kelly was urging Jamie not to reveal any more, and both children's play was less free on the rare occasions when I saw them together. I was becoming aware that one therapist could not meet both children's needs. Kelly reacted with relief when I suggested it would be good for her to have someone special. She responded well to the therapist to whom I referred her, and slowly began the painful process of revealing her own experience of abuse.

When Jamie realized this was happening, he was amazed at Kelly's change of position. He began to use the abuser's name in sessions with me, though he still needed to work through meta-phor rather than direct discussion. One of the images he loved to use was that of a top. Sometimes it represented his courage, with its colours waxing and waning, waxing and waning, as he moved the plunger that controlled its spinning. Sometimes he said it was Little Seal's power, and he spun it with intense energy, then 'gave it' to all Little Seal's protectors. Sometimes, we went down to the beach to let the wind help us play. On one of these occasions we took a helium-balloon male body Jamie had made and let the wind take it careering drunkenly up into the sky. Jamie (ever conscious of the world of nature) asked me what way was the wind blowing and where would it take 'the bad man'. It happened that it was a north wind and the balloon man was heading for the South Pole, a destination that made Jamie laugh. He also laughed when we took 'the spanking machine' to the beach. It was in the form of a windmill, powered by the bobbing up-and-down actions of a man, whose backside was vigorously kicked by the hind legs of an energetic horse. When the wind was strong, the action was hilariously fast. After that, Jamie would run along the line of the breaking waves, holding aloft his friend the Flying Fish (a wind-sock as large as himself). The active, physical engagement with these colourful symbols helped to deepen their impact.

I would have liked to have been able to continue working with Jamie, but shortly after the period when he began to use real names and refer to a few real situations, I had to travel in the course of my work. It was necessary to refer Jamie to a colleague. His new therapist has a wonderful playroom and, more importantly, large reserves of wisdom, love and experience. The work of healing this severely traumatized little boy and his sister is continuing. The parents, as well as the therapist, are involved in the slow and patient process of freeing them from the intense fear and trapped rage that are stunting their personal development at this stage. A balance needs to be restored. Cooke (1996) refers to the need for 'fine tuning' between the individual and the social world. Her research (1978, 1996) confirms both the capacity of the individual to change and the fact that change takes place within a framework of interconnected social relationships.

> The human person is constantly evolving and this evolutionary process is strongly influenced not only by the choices made by the individual, but also by those made by others – all others. Persons are 'human becomings' rather than 'human beings'. They are 'becomings' in an interdependent web of being. They are indeed their own co-creators as well as being co-creators of other humans. They can change. They can also choose the direction and tempo of that change – but change they do – continuously, and imperceptibly, for better or for worse.
>
> (Cooke 1996:512)

She goes on to discuss the effects of trauma on this evolutional change process.

> Human life could not exist on this planet without the cosmos being finely tuned to the physical aspects of its needs. The human person needs the social world also to be finely tuned to him or her if growth is to occur. Inner personal growth is a relational event. If intrapersonal change is precipitated too rapidly due to trauma for example, the individual's sense of self and others becomes too diffuse and he or she loses his or her 'bearings'. If development is arrested through a lack of interpersonal fine tuning on the part of significant others, fixation can occur. The change that ensues is resistance to growth. Growth cannot start again until at least some other 'fine tunes' to that person and he/she learns to respond.
>
> (*ibid*)

Alice Miller (1990) speaks strongly on the effects of abuse for children who are not given this help. Using anecdotal evidence, she describes the long-term effects for children who, through lack of appropriate help, are forced to suppress their emotions in response to abusive trauma.

> Dissociated from the original cause, their feelings of anger, helplessness, despair, longing, anxiety, and pain will find expression in destructive acts against others (criminal behaviour, mass murder) or against themselves (drug addiction, alcoholism, prostitution, psychic disorders, suicide).
>
> (Miller 1990:168)

Such clinically based opinion is backed by a growing body of research supporting the view that physical and sexual abuse have cyclical repercussions and long-term effects (Freeman-Longo 1990; Mullen *et al.* 1988; Finkelhor *et al.* 1989; Singer 1989; Browne and Finklehor 1986; Beitchman *et al.* 1992 – among others).

There is now widespread recognition of sexually abused children's need for immediate therapy, and many advances have been made in recent times to assist children to reveal abuse, where it occurs. Society has reached a point where significant sectors have joined forces to work towards the elimination of such a destructive, hidden crime. Jamie's story, however, highlights one of the stumbling blocks that has not yet been removed. The rules of evidence as presently used in the criminal court make it almost impossible for a very young child's statements to be strong enough to carry weight in a court hearing. The child's status as a competent witness is frequently discounted. It is beyond the scope of this book to analyse in depth the situation regarding witness competence and differing legal expectations for adults and children in the matter of truth-telling. Bussey (1992) does this competently, with a timely reliance on modern research rather than on old, discredited theories still cited inappropriately. She quotes the findings of Goodman, Hirschman and Rudy (1987) which support the view that children as young as three actually *resist* leading questions that go against the truth. They are *not* open to adults who try to obtain a false report of abuse. Meanwhile, as long as the abusers of young children remain secure in the knowledge that they are highly likely to escape conviction, the problem is perpetuated and these children remain vulnerable targets.

The challenge for our times consists in finding a way to modify court-room procedure so that children's evidence carries due weight. This modification needs to include the provision of highly specialized training for judges and advocates handling such cases. There is a gap in this area at present, and it can be reflected, for example, in the manner in which even videotaped evidence is handled. As one colleague of mine put it, 'We need to tackle the arena in which the court spectacle is played, rather than the rules of the ball game'. For no matter what changes we make in terms of the legislation, the implementation of the law is ultimately highly dependent on the attitudes, value judgments and knowledge-base of the judge and, to a lesser degree, of the police and lawyers involved in the hearing. The scales of justice need to be equally weighted for children and adults. It is not simply a matter of vengefulness against perpetrators of abuse, *it is a matter of breaking the cycle.* In the final analysis, that comes down to the question of how strongly are our governments committed to such a task? They will tinker with the system, from time to time, especially when they believe the voters want to see signs of action. But in its detail the task is huge, and the finance involved is enormous, affecting, as it does, so many levels of government – health, welfare, justice and finance. Perhaps the final question is really, 'How strongly is *society* committed to the task?' For 'the law' embraces much more than pieces of legislation. It includes all those sections of our society that are interwoven with it and on which its successful implementation depends. That web includes the will of the people, on whose votes our law-makers depend.

We have a long way to go before we find answers to the complex legal issues that are at present impeding the course of justice for many children and, as a consequence, perpetuating the problem. But questions are at least being openly raised, and research is increasingly providing the hard data that is needed to support anecdotal evidence. We have behind us centuries of neglect of this problem. It is therefore not surprising that great difficulties are encountered by those attempting to work towards systems-based solutions. But understanding of the obstacles is progressing and the work continues to be done.

14

AMANDA

Let us move back now to the world of direct experience, as revealed by a young girl whose story closes this section of the book. She had an unusual ability to create image after image that released hidden emotions and activated healing energy. Although her life was caught up in the mesh of the wider social system, with all its complexities, she moved in freedom in this therapy session. She has the power to draw us back swiftly to the expanses of metaphor-charged play. We need to re-enter that space.

Like many of the children with whom I work, Amanda's early childhood had been marked by disruption and periods of living with temporary care-givers. She was now thirteen years old and her foster-mother, Vicki, was going through the preliminary red tape to adopt her. Amanda's parents had been alcoholics and they had separated when she was a small child. She was only six when her mother died; they were alone in the house and Amanda found the body. She had displayed some regressive behaviour in recent months and Vicki thought she was disturbed by the fact that the adoption agency was trying to locate her father to obtain his consent.

At the time of the session described here, Amanda had been to see me twice before. Nothing of deep significance emerged in these two sessions. What came out next surprised me.

When she comes, in Amanda says immediately, 'Today I'm going to make a play for Vicki.'
B. 'That sounds good. Help me get the toys out.'
Amanda is excited, playful in an exaggerated way – hyperactive. She

chooses her favourites. Koala gets exaggerated cuddles. She hugs and kisses Panther. 'You're my husband!' *She throws Slippery Sam the Frog wildly to the ceiling several times. She picks up the Zany Doll and jiggles her, laughing.*

B. 'She looks a bit like you. You're both in very colourful clothes and you're in your 'Amanda-as-high-as-a-kite' mood.'

B and Amanda both laugh and Amanda goes on clowning.

B. 'Shall we make up a story about a girl like you? A girl who's lived in lots of places and now has at last found somewhere where she can be happy?'

A. *[Enthusiastically]* 'Yes! Let's make a time warp. . . . But I don't know where to begin.'

B. *[Sings]* 'Let's start at the very beginning.'

A. *[Excited]* 'I know that song!'

B nods. Amanda sings and B joins in: 'Let's start at the very beginning – a very good place to start.'

A. 'We'll start with me as a baby.'

B. 'Okay. Choose something to be this baby.'

Amanda chooses a baby doll and lies it down.

A. 'I'm being attacked by a dog.'

B. 'Choose the dog. . . . Make it happen.'

From then on, Amanda moves with speed, her freewheeling imagination leaping from image to image. The dog attacks the baby savagely.

B. *[Takes the role of horrified onlooker.]* 'Oh! . . . Somebody! . . . Who's looking after this baby? Where are her parents?'

A. *[Matter-of-factly]* 'They're down the pub.'

B. 'Choose the parents. . . . Put them at the pub.'

A chooses two clowns, and sits them on the floor a short distance away.

A. 'Now this is me when I'm a little bit older.' *[She chooses a slightly larger doll.]* 'Oh, her arm's fallen off . . . she got attacked by a lion.'

She makes this happen, then interrupts the ferocious growls and pounces.

'But it's all right. The Fairy Godmother's there.'

B. 'Oh! . . . Fairy Godmother? . . . Find the Fairy Godmother.'

Amanda rummages around. She laughs . . . and holds out a wooden duck.

A. 'You'll have to do. You can be the Fairy God-Duck.' *[B and Amanda both laugh.]*

B decides to use the Fairy God-Duck as a wisdom figure through which

Amanda's own inner wisdom can be assessed. Later, Wise Owl is also given this role.

B. 'Hello, Fairy God-Duck. What are you doing here?'

A. *[As Fairy God-Duck]* 'I'm here to look after her.'

B. 'Oh, that's good. Tell me, what do you think of her parents, leaving her to be attacked like this?'

A. *[As Fairy God-Duck]* 'They should be punished ... and their punishment is that they'll be split up.'

She tosses the Father to the end of the room, leaving the Mother where she is.

B. *[To A]* 'Let's see what Wise Owl thinks about this.' *[A gets Owl].*

B. 'And what does Owl say to Amanda?'

A. *[A bit shyly]* 'Always let your conscience be your guide.' *['That's from Pinocchio', she says to B in an aside. B nods.]* 'And don't let any of this harm you.'

Amanda's tone has changed. She is deeply reflective. B tunes in to this, with her body language and her words.

B. 'That's very wise, Owl. . . . **Very** wise!'

A. *[Suddenly]* 'I'm going to change the story of my childhood! Let's say my mother does not have an alcoholic problem any more.'

B is caught off guard, but she picks up the mood of strong determination. She mirrors Amanda's body language, accentuating it, striding around the stage, shouting: 'I'm going to CHANGE the story of my childhood!'

Amanda makes the mother attack the lion and try to rouse the doll representing Amanda by slapping her face and crying: 'Wake up! Wake up!'

B is reminded of the circumstances surrounding the death of Amanda's mother. She wonders if Amanda will go on to similar memory associations, but she keeps these wonderings to herself. There is no response from the doll in Amanda's play for some time. Much slapping and shaking goes on till the doll finally is made to sit up. Amanda suddenly switches the story.

A. 'Now we're going shopping.'

B. *[Doubling, and clowning around the idea of going shopping]* 'Shopping? ... mm ... shopping.' *[She holds out an imaginary shopping basket and leads A on a jaunty walk through the streets.]* 'Where are we?'

A. 'We're at Myer's . . . looking down at all the toys.'

B. 'Oh . . . so we must be high up. . . . Where are we?'

A. 'We're on the escalator.'

B *clowns around this and leaps on to the table. Amanda follows. Together they look down at the toys, excited, laughing, happy.*

A. 'And my mother buys all the toys for me.'

B. 'ALL the toys? ALL of them?' [*She doubles for A, joyfully gathering armfuls of toys.*] 'Oh, thank you, **thank you**, Mummy!'

A. 'And then she hears the price and she falls over.'

She makes the clown doll fall. Then she gets the doll representing herself to pick her up and stagger off home carrying her. She's talking to herself while she's doing this, describing her actions. Then she reverses it, making the mother pick up the child and carry her very tenderly in her arms. The two dolls are made to lie down together, with the mother holding the child protectively.

B registers the importance of this enactment for Amanda. She decides to heighten this moment with a verbal description of what she has observed.

B. 'How lovely . . . she's being a mother to you. . . . Before, you were trying to mother her . . . and it was a struggle, because you were too small to carry her properly.'

This is a very tender scene, which A suddenly interrupts. She has the mother fall down.

A. 'Now she falls down the stairs.'

She makes the doll representing herself shake the mother doll vigorously. She slaps her face repeatedly.

A. 'Mummy! Mummy! Wake up. Wake up.' [*Matter-of-factly*] 'We'll get the ambulance.' [*She goes to an imaginary telephone.*] 'Please come . . . my mother won't wake up.' [*She moves back towards B and again speaks matter-of-factly*] 'Now she's in the ground.'

B. 'Can you put her there?'

Amanda lies the doll on her back a little distance to the left. She begins a shovelling movement.

A. 'Now we shovel the dirt.'

B doubles, sensing Amanda's mood, feeling the rhythm. She sings as they both shovel, and the song has a lullaby quality, with B, as therapist, taking on an additional nurturing role, ensuring that A's concept of death will not be left solely with the harsh realism of the spade imagery.

B.   We'll shovel the dirt. . . . We'll shovel the dirt.
        We'll shovel the warm brown, soft brown dirt.

We'll make her safe, within the earth,
We'll make her safe within the warm brown earth.'

A. [*Still matter-of-factly*] 'Now we tread it in.' [*She walks up and down with steady, treading feet.*]

B. [*With change in melody, sings*]

Amanda will smooth the warm brown earth.
With her colourful feet she'll tread the soft brown earth.
She'll make her safe. She'll keep her warm.

B uses the Zany Doll to double, her multicoloured feet moving alongside Amanda's bright socks.

With her colourful, colourful, colourful treading feet.
In the earth, In the earth,
In the earth to which she has returned.

B smiles at Amanda as she brings the song to a close. She has seen the look of peace on her face. It seems like a good time to stop.

A. [*Suddenly*] 'And now Amanda's a bit more grown up. She's got a sister called Beganda who shows her how to look after babies.'

She chooses a doll to represent Beganda and makes her fuss with the baby.

B. 'Oh, hello Beganda.' [*in a tone of surprise*] 'How nice to meet you.'

A. [*As Beganda*] 'Now you hold her, Amanda.' [*She passes the doll.*] 'And change her nappy.' [*A does this with great dexterity and motherliness.*]

B. 'You're going to be a very good mother some day, Amanda. How lovely that you have this big sister you can learn from.'

Amanda nods and puts the baby down to sleep, again very expertly.

A. 'And now Amanda-Beganda's gone to live with Vicki.'

Just then the doorbell rings. It is Vicki returning. B and Amanda laugh.

B. 'Well, what do you know? The woman herself, coming just in time.' [*She goes to the door.*] 'Come in Vicki. Amanda's been making a marvellous story for you. . . . Will you tell it to her, Amanda?'

Vicki sits down, settling into her chair as if she's at the theatre.

V. 'Sounds good. . . . I'd love a story.'

A. [*Talking quickly, pointing quickly*] 'It's a time warp of my life. That's me when I'm a baby and a dog attacks me and my parents are at the pub. And that's me a bit more grown up and a lion attacks me and the Fairy God-Duck [*she laughs*] says my parents have to split up as punishment.' [*She stops.*]

B. 'And she made up a wonderful bit where her mother didn't have an alcohol problem and where they had happy times together.'

Amanda climbs on to Vicki's lap and buries her head in her shoulder. Vicki responds calmly, sensibly, without words – supportive but not sentimental.

B. 'And then she made up a most beautiful bit in the story. It touched my heart. She had her mother falling down the stairs and dying, and then she put her in the ground and told me to help her shovel the dirt. . . . And we did that . . . and I sang a song . . . and Amanda trod the earth in to make it safe and warm . . . and we finished our song.'

While B speaks she's kneeling in front of them with her hands on their arms, completing the circle their three bodies make. Vicki's eyes are on hers, and they show she's deeply moved. She sees the metaphorical significance of the story.

B. 'I think it's the most beautiful story a girl has ever made with me. I shall always remember it.'

Vicki increases her embrace of Amanda just slightly. She rocks her a tiny bit, and gives a small, matter-of-fact, but very tender pat to her back.

V. 'Yes . . . it was beautiful . . . it touched my heart too.'

B. 'And then you came in just as we got to the bit in the story where Amanda comes to live with you.' [*She stands up.*] 'Just in time to watch us celebrate. . . . Shall we celebrate, Amanda-Beganda? Celebrate your new life?' [*B laughs as she holds out her hand to A.*]

Amanda moves quickly into celebration mood. Together they clown and fool, dancing right through all the rooms of the cottage where B works, while B sings:

'And she lived happily ever after – happily every after – HAPPILY – HAPPILY – HAPPILY!! – EVER – AFTER!'

They both descend in a curtsey in front of Vicki. Laughing, all three embrace, acknowledging not only the joyful ending but also the deep importance of the work Amanda has just done.

In this session, Amanda demonstrated her ability to move swiftly (and, to the therapist, sometimes disconcertingly) to what was at the heart of her confusion – her need to complete her grieving process. She needed to grieve for the mother who actually died.

And she needed to grieve for the mother she never had. Above all, she needed to bury the Dream Mother so that she could be more fully open to a life of hope with a woman who wants to adopt her and whom she already loves and trusts, as her new mother.

As director, my task had been to facilitate the production of a drama. This included assisting Amanda to set up visually evocative scenes through clear directives (e.g. 'Choose something to be this baby', and later, referring to her mother: 'Can you put her there?'). It was vital at this stage not to intrude my own ideas but to follow what was coming from her. At a later point, when I wanted to deepen my own knowledge of what was going on, I used Wise Owl as the clarifier. At the same time, I was intending to put Amanda in touch with her own wisdom. 'Let's see what Wise Owl thinks about this?' . . . 'What does Wise Owl say to Amanda?' The reply that came to her provided a connecting bridge for her next leap into exploratory play. She went on immediately: 'I'm going to change the story of my childhood.' She then created the Dream Mother, fantasizing a delightful mother–child relationship. Using the psychodramatic tools of concretizing, mirroring, maximizing, doubling at appropriate moments in our play (for Amanda had made it clear it was 'our' play), I worked all the time to enable her to keep releasing her extraordinary spontaneity.

I have found, in working with children, that these methods also have an unintended secondary effect, assisting me to keep up with the swift-moving nature of some children's play while holding concurrently to the diagnostic role of the therapist. For example, when Amanda decided she wanted to change the story of her childhood, a combination of mirroring and maximizing led me to capture her mood as I strode around shouting 'I'm going to CHANGE the story of my childhood!' This enabled me to recover from the surprise of Amanda's sudden shift in her enactment at the very moment when I was tuning in to the strong feeling she was experiencing. The psychodramatic tools I was using performed this double task in a way that allowed the play to move on smoothly, with therapist and child remaining in harmony. It was similar with Amanda's extremely unexpected statement, 'Now we're going shopping', straight after a scene I thought might lead to a re-enactment of her mother's death. Keeping my thoughts to myself (for they were *my thoughts*) I doubled and clowned around the idea of going shopping, helping to maintain and extend Amanda's psychodramatic energy. At the same time, I was enabled to recover from my surprise and to follow her into this much more light-hearted role with barely a second's pause. If I had interrupted earlier (with some psychodramatic intervention aimed at accentuating the implications of A's action), I would have prevented the very touching scene that subsequently emerged, of a small child staggering under the burden of a help-less adult – a very powerful metaphor for the nurturing, respon-sible role a child often assumes in the web of daily life with an alcoholic parent. In Amanda's case, there was no need for me to highlight this metaphor at the time, for her own creative play moved swiftly forward to another extraordinary tender and evocative scene.

Her lack of fear in following what opened in her play kept the gateway between spontaneity and creativity open right through-out the session. I needed a similar fearlessness as I followed.

This collection of stories could well end here. Amanda's story illustrates one of the most important concepts in psychodrama. Antony Williams, in his book *The Passionate Technique*, describes it well:

> In spontaneity the 'two selves' – the conscious analytic teller and the unconscious doer – come together so that they func-tion as one harmonious whole. Action flows smoothly and freely; action and evaluation of action is automatic and hence unproblematic.
>
> (Williams 1989:11)

For Amanda, this integration took place in the context of swiftly moving, self-delighting play. Painful truths were actually faced and dealt with, but untraumatically. Insights came, and all the while her creative energy kept exploding into spontaneous play.

Part III

CONNECTIONS

Photo: Linda Gallus

15

WORKING WITH RESISTANCE

He instantly climbed up into a large tree, the branches of which spread out so close and thick that only one small opening was left. The tree itself grew at the foot of a sort of isolated rock, considerably higher than the tree and so steep that it could not be easily ascended.

(*The Arabian Nights*; 'Ali Baba and the Forty Thieves')

Not all children move with imaginative freedom and trust. Not all children come to the therapist at a point where buried pain or fear is ready to emerge spontaneously through metaphoric play, and some children cannot play at all. Let us turn our attention, for a moment, to them and to the patient, waiting game involved in reaching them. For each child must be approached within a context that is comprehensible to him or to her, and the path to communication with each child is unique. It is not opened up by any single, simple, 'Open sesame' formula. The therapist can often use the methods described in preceding chapters (and then the communication is rapid and powerful), but sometimes there is a need to keep exploring a variety of approaches – testing, discarding, inventing – until the way in has been found.

Are there any patterns in the type of resistance one can encounter? There are probably many. I shall confine the discussion here to patterns I have observed among the group of children referred to me. In this way speculation can be reined in, with examples from life tying it to reality. It is worth noting, however, that this is a somewhat biased sample, as many of the children I see have been sent simply because they are difficult to reach.

The first group that comes to mind includes children whose lives had been disrupted again and again, usually within the public welfare system. They had lived in institutions for varying lengths of time, and had often been moved from one foster home to another as 'placements' had 'broken down'. (Note the significance of the jargon used within that system. The children must have experienced a chaotic lack of control of their own lives as they were 'placed', and a great deal was 'broken' each time a move became necessary.) There was often great uncertainty within them as they waited for news of the next home to be found for them. And there was often little continuity in terms of personnel handling particular children's cases. A very fat file grew as worker after worker presented a report before moving on to another job setting. The next worker was left to sift and interpret facts from a proliferation of paperwork. Time pressures often led to the overlooking of important connecting threads in the mass of detail.

Meanwhile, the children coped as resourcefully as possible, learning a degree of cynicism and wariness towards this ever-changing parade of adults – seeing the social worker sometimes as a sort of servant who 'does things for us', and often as a power-figure who could turn their lives upside down if too much was revealed. They developed a certain need to control adults, for fear of losing control of their own lives. They became adept at this in a therapy session. For they had known a procession of therapists too, and they were very experienced in guarding their private space. Two of the children in my mind as I write were highly intelligent: I suspect they were aware of the power of the puppets to move them into uncharted territory. Their conscious, ever-watchful intellects were on the alert to prevent any self-revealing play that could shift the power-base away from their own control. They needed to feel they were the sole arbiters of their lives, and that the shape of the therapy session was entirely in their hands. The uncomfortable pressures in those pre-conscious parts of their being, for which they had no name, needed to be rigidly contained. These children tested my ingenuity to the full as I sought ways to reach them without violating their defences.

With one of them, this has involved accepting the smoke-screen she creates when she refuses to do anything but play school (for her, a wonderfully safe device that keeps me away from any of the real issues in her life). She sets up the game with herself as the teacher and with me as the child. We later reverse roles. Through-

out the course of our long therapeutic relationship we have established considerable mutual understanding. It is possible she finds
useful material in the psychodramatic techniques I occasionally
use in this game, causing her to laugh as I defy the teacher's
demands for conformity, by running around choosing puppets to
represent the topics she's avoiding, and pushing them under my
chair. 'I always sit on these, Miss', I say. 'It's all right. No-one can
see them if I sit on them.' And I squash my chair on top of them
and then sit demurely, if somewhat precariously, ready to answer
the life-irrelevant questions she asks in her role as teacher. When
we reverse roles, she doesn't take up the challenge by focussing
on any of the issues she's concealing. The puppets remain simply
a non-threatening allusion of mine to her need to push problems
down. She is aware of the challenge existing side-by-side with
acceptance of her need. In time, and on her own terms, she may
allow one or other of these issues to surface briefly. Meanwhile,
the game of school continues, and I must be patient.

With another of these children, the way in is through stories. In
the period where she was most resistant, we played the 'instant
stories' game, taking turns to tell brief, unrehearsed stories and
illustrating them with the puppets and other props in the room.
Gradually, without any conscious help from her, I formed some
tentative hypotheses as to what was at the heart of her problem. I
created one story that she loved, using several small birds' nests
that I had collected. The story revolved around a beautifully colourful little bird that was constantly tipped out of its nest. The
shock of each upheaval was great, but the worst of them brought
a sudden and devastating separation from the gardener who had
become her dearest friend. Adroitly side-stepping any personal
implications, the child enjoyed the story for its own sake. 'That
was beautiful', she said. 'Why did you stop?' I had no intention of
stopping, so I promised to continue the story at her next visit.

By then, I had sharpened my focus to address some deeper
issues. The story I gave her was a quite elaborate tale, of a bird
called Bellissima Splendoribus, who became very agitated if
anyone suggested she was not flying absolutely perfectly. She
screamed abuse at the Sun and beat her wings against his face
when he tried to talk to her about it. So great was her agitation
that the Sun became worried and talked it over with the Moon
that night when they were changing the guard. The Moon promised to make sure the little bird was all right, but was not certain

she'd be able to see her. (For the Moon knew Bellissima had a way of fending off anyone who tried to talk to her about personal matters. She would drop down over her nest a curtain of leaves that she had spent years weaving. It was woven so tightly that not a chink of light could get past it, and when she hid behind it, no-one could see her.)

The story I told the child was long, and together we acted it out, setting up chairs and cushions and radiant scarves to represent the Sun and the Moon. We slid them around the room as day gave way to night, and the child took great delight in causing Bellissima to hover over the pond (a large mirror) where she was anxiously reassuring herself that she was indeed beautiful, no matter what the Sun said. The child, by now, was highly involved in the story, and when finally Bellissima asked the Moon to help her find her own special path in the sky, she had her take the curtain of leaves with her as they set off, looking for the thermals where Bellissima would learn to soar. As they crossed the ocean, the child caused Bellissima to drop the curtain into the sea, for it was hampering her flight.

We will continue the story in later therapy sessions, and, no doubt, I will sometimes have the bird dart down to rescue her precious safety curtain, for it has been a valued defence for too long in her life to be so lightly discarded. And, no doubt, Bellissima will still have to grapple with the perceived contradiction between her knowledge of her own inner beauty and the Sun's insistence that she has not perfectly mastered the art of soaring. It has taken months for our therapy sessions to reach this point, and I imagine it will take quite some time yet before the child can deal directly with the issues that are troubling her. Perhaps they are not yet ready to surface, for they had their origins in a background story that is complex and possibly forgotten.

Another group of children displaying lack of freedom with the puppets could be described as children who were guarding a secret. In each case, it was a secret connected with sexual abuse. They, too, carefully avoided anything too personal, and many, many weeks of joining their inconsequential play were needed before the suppressed material could begin to emerge. One such very young child (a four-year-old) had strong imaginative powers, and in the early sessions he enjoyed all his play, linking it to favourite television characters. The television stereotypes were gradually discarded, and his play eventually included locking me in gaol. This was a little dark area he had discovered he could create by shutting four doors. A much earlier session had been spent in this same dark place, in an atmosphere of total serenity and trust, with his little cheek resting against mine as he ordered me to lie there for the whole of the therapy session. The space he had made had no connotations of gaol at that time, but seemed to be part of a trust-testing process. Several months of seemingly tangential play preceded his disclosure of the details of his sexual abuse. His foster parents and I needed both patience and trust in the therapeutic process as he released aggression and fear. His foster father and mother were excellent in their understanding of this little boy, for whom there were probably years of damage to undo. We are all still working on the task.

Now we come to a third group, the nature of whose resistance involved lack of rapport with the puppets and discomfort with unstructured play. This group included children whose imaginative powers were limited, for a variety of reasons. At one end of the scale was Carl, a nine-year-old boy, whose stage of development and life interests were tied up with very active sports, and whose language skills were not highly developed. Storytelling had no interest for him, and the puppets were just unappealing toys. Life was very action-centred, and it was understood in concrete rather than metaphorical terms. Communication with him had to follow a different path, involving a changing array of action-based techniques that provided structure and that were not linked with the toys. We were able to achieve a break-through one day in our efforts to uncover the source of some disabling, displaced anxiety in his life that had emerged after he disclosed to his mother details of sexual abuse by a neighbour. He had developed an obsessive fear that he could cause harm to people – even kill them – through simple acts such as accidentally hitting a car with a tennis ball when playing, etc.

The technique I developed with Carl involved throwing out on paper any and every word that came into his head, forgetting the niceties of spelling and meaning and letting the words come freely. I wanted to see if writing was a medium we could use to explore his confused thoughts. The word-throwing technique was a new one that suddenly sprang into my mind. Because Carl was experiencing a high level of anxiety about life in general, I needed to set him free from fear of 'getting it wrong' – I needed to release his ability to make free associations. We relaxed into fun, as I urged him to go faster and faster, like a juggler with many balls in the air at once, having no thought of rules that might govern this game. He filled a page with joyfully chaotic scribble and grew progressively more relaxed. I then gave him a clean sheet of paper and told him to throw on to the page any word that came to him when he thought about his worries – to throw them first, whether they made sense or not. 'Why', 'tree', 'took' came on to the page. I asked him if the words had any significance for him. Immediately he realized they were connected with the known sexual abuse that was central to his problem, and discussion of the particular incident to which they referred brought new and unexpected insights. The hitherto inexplicable anxiety that had been displaced to a range of unconnected situations suddenly found its true focus. He remembered an incident when his abuser took him behind a tree. That night he suddenly became aware that he was afraid he could have AIDS. The fear at last had a name. He remembered details of his abuse that had been repressed and he was able to talk about it. He expressed over-whelming relief in a drawing he made at that time. Frankl (1959) describes the effect of being able to define an elusive source of distress: 'Emotion, which is suffering, ceases to be suffering as soon as we form a clear and precise picture of it' (Frankl 1959: 117). In later therapy sessions, Carl worked quite quickly through many of the tangled emotions he'd been repressing, using draw-ing, talking and the word-throwing game. He then expressed a wish to leave it all behind as he got on with the rest of his life. I suspect he may need to address some of the issues again at a much later stage.

At the other end of the scale in this group was a young child whose inability to use the puppets was linked with traumatic experiences, rather than to the pragmatism of his own nature. He had suffered gross sexual abuse some years earlier, and he still had vivid memories of the perpetrators dressing up in costumes reminiscent of my toys. His imagination has been shackled by fear, and he remains quite unable to free it at present. I am still in the process of seeking a therapeutic medium that will unlock him a little. It is possible that the vivid fluidity of paint may help him find healing. But introducing him to it will need to be a gentle, careful process that takes into account his fear of the unfamiliar.

Klein (1932) sees inhibition in play as an extremely common neurotic symptom.

> It may be thought from what has been said that all we have to do in order to analyse a child is to put toys in front of it, and that it will then immediately begin to play with them in an uninhibited and easy fashion. That is not at all what happens.
>
> (Klein 1932:33)

The therapist's task in engaging a child is much more complex than that. Klein reminds us of the underlying causes of a child's blockages:

> we sometimes encounter resistances which are hard to overcome. This most usually means that we have come up against a child's anxiety and sense of guilt belonging to deeper layers of its mind.
>
> (*ibid*:9)

Some summarizing reflections will provide a connecting thread between the three groups described above and the therapist's admission of the complexity of the problems involved. In working with resistance, the therapist has three main tasks:

1 To respect the child's defence mechanisms – acknowledging their existence; offering a gentle challenge where appropriate; never forcing a way past them.
2 To develop increasingly refined hypotheses, based on observation, as to what might lie at the centre of this child's difficulties.
3 To search, with ever-sharpening accuracy, for the right therapeutic medium for each particular child – bearing in mind the child's cultural background, stage of development, particular interests and skills; and working always within the context of the therapeutic relationship. (The story of Bellissima, for example, grew out of a relationship with the child for whom it was created. It took into account her passionate interest in natural history. For a child who had no such interests, a story about issues of control, insecurity and fear of criticism would require an entirely different setting before it would resonate with therapeutic power.)

Working with children demands great flexibility. Their resistances call on the psychodrama director's ingenuity even more fully than do their flights of metaphorical play – challenging, demanding alternative pathways, calling for patient, unremitting persistence. And all the while, the therapist is acknowledging the need to adapt the psychodramatic techniques normally used with adults. Working with children is very different from working with adults. It may be well to spend some time on that difference in the following chapter, and to compare classical psychodrama with this particular adaptation for children.

Photo: Linda Gallus

16

PSYCHODRAMA AND CHILD THERAPY

> . . . you don't need a ball to play ball!
> Come, I'll toss the sun to you, catch it.
> (Moreno)

Moreno provides a useful focus for a comparison of classical psychodrama with an adaptation for children, with his clear description of the role of the director in classical psychodrama:

> [The director] has three functions: producer, therapist and analyst . . . as producer, to be on the alert to turn every clue which the subject offers into action, to make the line of the production one with the life-line of the subject, and never to let the production lose rapport with the group . . . as therapist attacking and shocking the subject . . . at times indirect and passive. As analyst, he may complement his interpretation by responses coming from informants in the group; husband, wife, parents, children.
>
> (Moreno 1946:c)

There are some obvious similarities between this description and the therapist's role outlined in earlier chapters. But there are also some clear differences. The first of these differences relates to the setting. The child therapy described here was not done in a group, with group members being chosen as auxiliary egos to act out characters in the child's story, and with the director maintaining a separate position. Instead, the characters were represented by puppets, animated by the child or by the therapist. As a result, the therapist had to move fluidly between the roles of director and auxiliary, maintaining the roles of producer, therapist and analyst while at the same time engaging fully in co-operative play as the child's auxiliary ego. This combination of roles and tasks, in an atmosphere of uninterrupted play, could only be achieved if the therapist flowed freely with all that emerged. This involved a certain receptiveness to the energies to be released in the therapy room and a trust in their power. In his discussion of the beginning of an interview, Max Clayton calls this preparatory time the 'creation of readiness'.

> A certain atmosphere can be created by the director in a few swift moments of time. It can be done very simply. It most certainly involves allowing time to stand still momentarily. You pause to realize the nature of your own being. That must be so for everything commences with being. Doing comes later.
>
> (Clayton 1991:5–6)

Speaking to the would-be director of a session with an adult, he says:

> This is my recommendation to you. Focus on the life-force in you and in the other person. Regard that life-force as a precious thing. See the life-force as an awesome thing since it contains within itself a creative power that is mightier than that of the atom. When I am able to do this I find that something grows within me.
>
> (*ibid*:6)

The process when working with children is similar. Entering intuitively into the therapeutic session that is about to begin, the director is open to its power and is not paralysed by fear of the unpredictable and the demands of moving from role to role in response to the child's play.

Let us return now to significant differences. Although Moreno's technique of 'attacking and shocking the subject' can result in deep insights for an adult protagonist, the therapist working with children must proceed more gently. Challenges can be made (and, indeed, need to be made at times), but some children can be devastated by the smallest overt criticism. Their response to a clumsy negative approach is instant withdrawal. Their protective mechanisms are activated, with the speed and finality of a switch-operated steel security door. They lose all spontaneity and all desire to engage in therapeutic play, and their trust in the director plummets to zero. Some examples will illustrate this need for care.

Jason was able to respond to my challenge of his victim role when it came via the helpless little monkey. But, even so, his face reflected his sense of shock. He needed that deep insight to be buttressed by an equally strong enactment of a more positive, life-enhancing role in his role repertoire. Mary Kate was able to accept the challenge to her hiding of hurtful truths only because she was approached with tenderness and love. The path to challenge for many of the other children was through the use of surprise tactics – a sudden introduction of a wisdom figure who would ask a pertinent question; or a sudden role reversal with a character in the enactment. In the atmosphere of our shared play and under the protection of metaphor, the children felt safe. They could absorb the insights without a sense that the director had exposed their secret fears or forced them to face unwanted truths. 'Attacking' and 'shocking' were not appropriate.

As for Moreno's comments on the director's use of extraneous material from relatives, there are again some clear differences. He is speaking of information-sharing that is part of the whole psychodramatic experience for the protagonist. It takes place within a group setting. It belongs in a dynamic process that takes words beyond themselves into the unpredictable realm of psychodramatic action. The therapy sessions described in this book were not held in a group context. Information was given by the parents in a separate session and was not part of the fantasy-laden play of the child. Chapter 3, entitled 'The Way In', gives some indication of the manner in which this information was received and the trust issues that were involved. After that initial sharing of background information, the children usually preferred to deal with sensitive material through metaphor. But through ongoing contact with the parents or care-givers, the therapist was often aware of important later events in the child's life. This knowledge illuminated the child's metaphorical play for the therapist, sensitizing her to respond more fully and more accurately, while still remaining within the context of fantasy. The description of the stripped therapy room in chapter 4 is a graphic example of the value of such extraneous information. Used sensitively, it complements the therapist's analysis of the play that is unfolding.

There is, perhaps, no need to say much about one final difference between classical psychodrama and this form of therapy. All the foregoing pages have revealed the children's major perception of the therapist as a playmate. They are invariably aware of the healing role that is also there, but the overwhelming experience for them is one of play. They leap swiftly from metaphor to metaphor, and their conscious minds do not pause to analyse or assess. The adult protagonist's self-aware search for new insights, with the director as trusted guide, belongs in a world they have not yet entered. They prefer to fly.

Photo: Bernadette Hoey

17

BEYOND THE BARRIERS

The sparrows were brighter than peacocks here,
And their dogs outran our fallow deer,
And honey bees had lost their stings,
And horses were born with eagles' wings.
(Browning: 'The Pied Piper')

The literature on psychodrama never adequately conveys the reality. It resembles a photograph. By holding a living, moving subject still, and focussing on a light-filled section of it, a photographer can draw attention to its beauty, or its intricacy or its dramatic intensity. But it is held in time, like a butterfly on a pin, caught in one particular moment. So, too, with the vibrant, ever-changing reality of the therapy sessions described here. It cannot be captured, no matter how graphically the sessions are described.

In my training workshops, an attempt is made to retain the dynamic interplay between therapist, child and puppet auxiliaries. An actor is trained to take on the role of the child, using a script that is as close to verbatim as possible. But that, too, is inadequate. We are repeating the words, and trying to replicate the movements, the expressions, the emotions of a moment that has already passed, whereas psychodrama is about the freshness and immediacy of the moment, experienced now. This re-enactment is closer to conventional theatre – a theatre Moreno describes as 'out of locus' (Moreno 1926:18). What does he mean?

In Morenian terms, everything that exists has its place of origin – its 'locus nascendi', and when removed from that place it loses something of its original essence. Moreno sees conventional theatre as far removed from the moment of a dramatic work's primary creation, and he links this with the reliance on fixed scripts and buildings that have a pre-determined function. To illustrate the difference between the 'theatre of spontaneity' and the stylized, fixed-in-time form of conventional theatre, Moreno uses the analogy of a flower that has been taken out of its locus (the place where it had its origin) and placed in a woman's hair. As we look at it there, we can lose all concept that its true locus is the bed where it grows into a flower (*ibid*:12). There is a tantalizing imprecision in Moreno's use of language here, and yet the concepts intrigue. Their central importance to the psychodramatic method is recognized by those who have experienced this form of therapy as protagonists. For this was the attitude to theatre that led Moreno to develop the very techniques that allow a person to re-enter the 'locus nascendi' of an original experience – the place where it was born, the place where it all began. In psychodrama, they live this experience with a depth of intensity which is different from that undergone by even the most brilliant actor using a fixed script.

When, in my workshops, I resort to using an established script, the audience is given some insight into a child's original creative energy. But much is lost. By reducing the unpredictable dynamism of a child's psychodramatic play to the printed word, or to the form of a re-enactment, one removes it from its locus, giving it a final, static state. It is therefore impossible to convey its essence fully. It has been taken out of the context where the child and the therapist were creators. Readers or workshop participants have been invited to be observers of an account, rather than active participants in a process as it unfolds. The child and the process are objects of study. They hold our attention in much the same way as the flower in the woman's hair. It is legitimate to study them, but the experience for a therapist will be different if this study leads on to using the method in a therapeutic setting. Then the experience will be closer to Moreno's description of the theatre of spontaneity. The therapy room will become 'a place where life is tested, the strong and the weak – by play. It is the place of truth without might' (*ibid*:26).

Therapist and child will be creators, set free from the constraints of time, and they will discover the fluidity of the barriers between conscious and unconscious.

For a continually creating mind, the distinction between

conscious and unconscious would not exist. A creator is like a runner for whom in the act of running the part of the road he has already passed and the part before him are qualitatively one.

(ibid:42)

Going down this road, in the company of a child, now following, now leading, now following again, is a journey of continual discovery.

Moreno began by observing children at play. His observations and experiences finally led him to the complexities and subtleties of psychodrama. Intrigued by all I had learned through psychodrama, I opened my mind to trace this unwritten progression of thought back to its origins. The children are continuing to teach me. We work in freedom. Much of what I have learned has come through moving beyond the barren restrictions of institutions. For too many years, they held me captive, the wings of my creativity clipped to safe proportions. The children set me free.

One day, when I was a child,

I was exploring the meandering path

of a little creek near my home. I came

upon a piece of string. It seemed

to have no end. I followed its trail,

along a stretch of grassland, over fences,

through thick scrub — for miles, it seemed —

becoming increasingly curious as I went. It

finally led me to a tall tree. My eyes

followed it, right up the trunk, to the highest branches

where a large and beautiful kite hung trapped.

Each child who responds to this form
of psychodrama sets free the kite,
causing it to soar aloft
in power.

BIBLIOGRAPHY

Axline, V. (1964) *Dibs In Search of Self*, London, Pelican

Beitchman, J. H., Zucker, K. J., Hood, J. E., da Costa, G. A., Akman, D. and Cassavia, E. (1992) 'Review of the long-term effects of child sexual abuse' in *Child Abuse and Neglect*, vol. 16: 101–118

Berg, W. K. and Berg, K. M. (1979) 'Psychophysiological development in infancy: state, sensory function and attention', in J. D. Osofsky (ed.) *Handbook of Infant Development*, New York, John Wiley & Sons

Bettleheim, B. (1976/1989) *The Uses of Enchantment*, New York, Vintage Books

Bray, M. (1991) *Poppies on the Rubbish Heap – Sexual Abuse: The Child's Voice*, Edinburgh, Canongate Press

Browne, A. and Finkelhor, D. (1986) 'Impact of child sexual abuse: a review of the research', *Psychological Bulletin*, vol. 99, no. 1: 66–77

Bussey, K. (1992)'The competence of child witnesses', in Calvert G., Ford A. and Parkinson, P. (eds) *The Practice of Child Protection – Australian Approaches*, Sydney, Hale and Iremonger

Clayton, G. M. (1991) *Directing Psychodrama: A Training Companion*, Caulfield, Australia, ICA Press

Cooke, P. B. (1978) 'Person perception and behaviour patterns: a clinical application of multidimensional analysis', unpublished PhD thesis, University of Western Australia

—— (1996)*Young People Who Offend: New Research and Application*, forthcoming

Emy, H. V. and Hughes, O. E. (1988) *Australian Politics: Realities in Conflict*, Melbourne, Macmillan

Erickson, M. (1958/1980) 'Paediatric hypnotherapy', in E. Rossi (ed.) *The Collected Papers of Milton H. Erickson on Hypnosis. Vol. 1: The Nature of Hypnosis and Suggestion*, New York, Irvington Publishers, Inc.

Erickson, M. and Rossi, E. (1976/1980) 'Two-level communication and the microdynamics of trance and suggestion', in E. Rossi (ed.) *The Collected Papers of Milton H. Erickson on Hypnosis. Vol. 1: The Nature of Hypnosis and Suggestion*, New York, Irvington Publishers, Inc.

—— (1979) *Hypnotherapy: An Exploratory Casebook*, New York, Irvington Publishers, Inc.

Fagan, J. and Shepherd, I. L. (eds) (1970/1972) *Gestalt Therapy Now*, Harmondsworth, Penguin

Field, T. M., Woodson, R., Greenberg, R. and Cohen, D. (1982) 'Discrimination and imitation of facial expressions by neonates', *Science*, vol. 218: 179–181

Finkelhor, D., Hotaling, T. P., Lewis, I. A. and Smith, C. (1989) 'Sexual abuse and its relationship to later sexual satisfaction, marital status, religion and attitudes', *Journal of Interpersonal Violence*, vol. 14, no. 4

Fogarty, J. (1993) *Protective Services for Children in Victoria*, Report to Victorian Government, Melbourne

Frankl, V. (1959) *Man's Search For Meaning*, New York, Pocket Books

Freeman-Longo, R. (1990) 'The evaluation and treatment of sexual offenders', paper presented at Conference: Sex Offenders – Management Strategies, for the Office of Corrections and Health Department, Victoria

Freud, S. (1905/1957) 'Fragment of an analysis of a case of hysteria', *Collected Papers*, vol. 3, London, Hogarth Press

Friedrich, O. (1983) 'What do babies know?' *Time*, 15 August, 48–55

Galin, D. (1974) 'Implications for psychiatry of left and right specialization', in *Archives of General Psychiatry*, vol. 31: 527–583

Goodman, G. S., Hirschman, J. and Rudy, L. (1987) 'Children's testimony: research and policy implications', in *Children as Witness: Research and Social Implications*. S. Ceci (Chair), Symposium presented at the Society for Research in Child Development, Baltimore, MD

Herman, J. L. (1992) *Trauma and Recovery*, London, HarperCollins

James, M. R. (trans.) (1930/1959) *Hans Andersen, Forty Two Stories*, London, Faber and Faber

Jung, Carl (1958) *Psyche and Symbol*, NewYork, Doubleday

—— (1934/1991) *The Archetypes and the Collective Unconscious*, Part 1, London, Routledge

—— (ed.) (1964) *Man and His Symbols*, New York, Doubleday

Keen, S. (1969/1973) *Apology for Wonder*, New York, Harper and Row

Kelly, G. A. (1955) *The Psychology of Personal Constructs*, vol. 1, New York, W. W. Norton & Co. Inc.

Klein, M. (1932/1989) *The Psychoanalysis of Children*, London, Virago Press

Kuhl, P. and Meltzoff, A. N. (1982) 'The bimodal perception of speech in infancy', *Science*, vol. 218: 1138–1141

Luria, A. (1973) *The Working Brain*, New York, Basic Books

MacKain, K., Studdert-Kennedy, M., Spieker, S. and Stern, D. N. (1981/1982) 'Infant perception of auditory–visual relations for speech', paper presented at the International Conference of Infancy Studies, Austin, TX

Mannoni, M. (1967/1970) *The Child, His Illness and the Others*, New York, Random House

Marineau, R. F. (1989) *Jacob Levy Moreno 1889–1974 Father of Psychodrama, Sociometry and Group Psychotherapy*, London, Routledge

Martinez, L. (1992/1993) In *Juvenile Justice: A New Focus on Prevention*, Washington, US Government Printing Office, Serial No. J–102–62

Mellon, N. (1992/1993) *Storytelling and the Art of Imagination*, Brisbane, Element Books Ltd

Meltzoff, A. N. and Moore, K. (1977) 'Imitation of facial and manual gestures by human neonates', *Science*, vol. 198: 75–78

Miller, A. (1990) *The Untouched Key*, London, Virago Press

Mills, J. C. and Crowley, R. J. (1986) *Therapeutic Metaphors for Children and the Child Within*, New York, Brunner/Mazel, Inc.

Moreno, J. L. (1926/1973) *The Theatre of Spontaneity*, New York, Beacon House

—— (1934/1953) *Who Shall Survive? A New Approach to the Problem of Human Interrelations*, New York, Beacon House

—— (1946/1980) *Psychodrama*, vol. 1, 4th edition with new introduction, New York, Beacon House (6th edition)

Moreno, J. L. and Moreno, F. B. (1944) 'Spontaneity Theory of Child Development', in *Psychodrama Monographs*, no. 8, New York, Beacon House

Mullen, P. E., Romans-Clarkson, S. E., Walton, V. A. and Herbison, G. P. (1988) 'Impact of sexual and physical abuse on women's mental health', *The Lancet*, vol. 1, no. 8590: 841–845

Nebes, R. (1977) 'Man's so-called minor hemisphere', in M. Wittock (ed.) *The Human Brain*, Englewood Cliffs, NJ, Prentice-Hall

Ornstein, R. (1978) 'The split and whole brain', *Human Nature*, vol. 1, no. (5): 76–83

Rogers, L., TenHouten, W., Kaplan, C. and Gardner, M. (1977) 'Hemispheric specialization of language : An EEG study of bi-lingual Hopi Indian children', *International Journal of Neuroscience*, vol. 8: 1–6

Rossi, E. L. (ed.) (1980) *The Collected Papers of Milton H. Erickson on Hypnosis, Vol. iv, Innovative Hypnotherapy*, New York, Irvington Publishers, Inc.

Salzberger-Wittenberg, I. (1970/1988) *Psycho-Analytic Insight and Relationships*, London, Routledge

Singer, K. (1989) 'Group work with men who experienced incest in childhood', *American Journal of Orthopsychiatry*, vol. 59, no. 3: 468–476

Smith, S. B. (1985) *Children's Story: Sexually Molested Children in Criminal Court*, Walnut Creek, CA, Launch Press

Stern, D. N. (1985) *The Interpersonal World of the Infant*, [New York], Basic Books Inc.

Williams, A. (1989) *The Passionate Technique* London, Routledge

Winnicott, D. W. (1971) *Therapeutic Consultations in Child Psychiatry*, New York, Basic Books

GLOSSARY

TERMS AND TECHNIQUES USED IN PSYCHODRAMA

act hunger the thrust towards the fulfilment of basic drives and impulses.

auxiliary ego (sometimes referred to simply as 'auxiliary') in classical psychodrama, a person from the group who takes on the role of a significant other, within a scene the protagonist has set up in the course of a psychodramatic exploration. As the term implies, this person is an assistant – to the director as well as to the protagonist. In the work described in this book, the puppets are used in this role, frequently acting metaphorically.

concretizing abstract ideas or verbal reminiscences are put into a visible form, by setting out scenes or by creating metaphorical representations.

director Moreno's name (taken from theatre vocabulary) for the therapist using psychodrama methods.

double in classical psychodrama, a person who plays the role, or some aspects of the role, of the protagonist. The double's task is to move alongside the protagonist and to identify as fully as possible with the thoughts, emotions, actions and words that are expressed or that lie hidden beneath the surface. In this adaptation for children, the puppets sometimes have a similar function.

enactment the reproduction of a scene that the protagonist wishes to explore, and an acting out of the event that includes a dramatization of previously unspoken thoughts, unacknowledged longings, hidden fears. Reality and the realm of the imagination work together.

first universe Moreno's term for that earliest period in an infant's life, before the capacity for image-building is strongly developed, when everything is experienced as real and only the present moment is significant.

locus nascendi the original location in which a thing first came into being.

maximizing involves an enlargement of small movements, low-key expressions of emotion or softly spoken words, till the enhanced dramatic action leads to a fuller and deeper experience for the protagonist.

mirroring a technique that involves the protagonist standing back to observe, while another person copies his/her behaviour – capturing the feeling behind it and sometimes consciously exaggerating it in order to arouse new levels of self-knowledge in the protagonist.

protagonist the principal actor in the therapeutic drama, the person whose life is being explored.

spontaneity (as defined by Moreno) a new and adeqate response to a new situation, or a new response to an old situation.

status nascendi the primary moment of creation.

AUSTRALIAN PLANTS AND ANIMALS

dingo wild dog, often thought to be native to Australia, but possibly introduced 4,000–5,000 years ago. Typically ginger in colour, with white points. Some black, with tan points. Alert, pricked ears and bushy tail. It can live in all the varied terrains that are part of the Australian landscape, including desert country.

echidna an interesting little animal (40–45 cm long) found only in

Echidna searching for ants in sandy soil

Australia and Papua New Guinea. An egg-laying mammal, it belongs in the order of *monotremata*, and its only close relative is the platypus. Both these animals represent an important stage in the evolutionary development of mammals, being the only survivors of their particular group. In the evolutional scale they are just one step up from reptiles. When disturbed, the echidna curls into a ball of radiating spines, or (if on soil) it digs below the surface, disappearing like a sinking ship. It's also capable of extending its spines and limbs to wedge itself into small spaces, such as rock crevices or hollow logs – apparently very effective survival strategies since it has avoided extinction over millions of years. Echidnas came into prominence shortly after the dinosaurs became extinct.

melaleuca an Australian native tree, growing to a height of up to eight metres, with papery bark and fine-twigged branches having a dense cover of needle-like leaves. In spring and summer, soft creamy blossoms appear, similar in shape to a bottlebrush.

INDEX

143